SALONS AND SPAS

ROCKPORT

SALONS AND SPAS

THE ARCHITECTURE OF BEAUTY ▪ JULIE SINCLAIR EAKIN

BEVERLY MASSACHUSETTS

ROCKPORT PUBLISHERS

First published in the United States of America by
Rockport Publishers, a member of
Quayside Publishing Group
100 Cummings Center
Suite 406-L
Beverly, MA 01915-6101
Telephone: 978.282.9590
Fax: 978.283.2742
www.rockpub.com

Library of Congress Cataloging-in-Publication Data available

ISBN-13: 978-1-59253-396-1
ISBN-10: 1-59253-396-5

10 9 8 7 6 5 4 3 2 1

Editor: Alicia Kennedy

Design: Dutton & Sherman Design

Cover image: Qiora Store and Spa by ARO
Photograph by David Joseph

Back cover image: LabulleKenzo by Emmanuelle Duplay
Photograph by Marc Abel

Printed in China

CONTENTS

INTRODUCTION

Beauty is ceasing to be an ugly word among architects. In leading design schools just ten years ago, few architecture students would have dared use the term to describe the merits of their work among a jury of serious practitioners, much less attempt to address the concept programmatically. But recent sightings of salons and spas in design magazines indicate this change is emblematic of our contemporary built reality. The presence of these projects can be attributed to the nature of capitalism: For beauty is currently exactly what the design market will bear. As consumers have become more educated about the potential for design to enhance—or detract from—their experience of the world, they are demanding that the places they visit to invest in their ideal of the beautiful reflect it as well. The accelerated buying power of women in the workplace mirrors the increased success of salons and, more recently, day spas, while the emergence of a men's beauty market in this century alone reveals an acceptance of professionally provided grooming as part of all of our daily lives. Architects are learning that stretching their creative muscles in the direction of salons and spas makes perfect fiscal sense, and they're also recognizing that these formerly overlooked venues provide them with a substantial workout. Designs for spaces of beauty today are as rigorously conceived as any other program.

Since long before John Keats wrote "Beauty is truth, truth beauty," the idea that genuine beauty is unadorned has been consistently promoted by poets—and just as consistently contradicted by many beauty professionals, one might suggest. But this, too, is changing. Beauty's emergence from behind closed doors to be addressed publicly in the design community means the old beauty parlor is being subjected to a significant makeover and replaced by its more "truthful" contemporary counterpart. Today, beauty is equated with well-being. Just as our desired transformations do not make us unrecognizable, but ultimately aim to reveal our more

The streamlined girl of today demands her beauty services in a shop harmonious with her own modernity.

Vogue, May 1921

essential, vital selves, the same may be said of the designs for the spaces of beauty gathered in this collection.ˈ

If successful architecture functions in part as a vessel to contain our activities, it may also reflect the way we perceive ourselves engaging in these endeavors. Currently, there are two strong forces being articulated in the designs for the spaces of beauty we've encountered, and they promote distinctly different desires: that of retreat and that of connection. This book has consequently been divided into dual categories displaying primarily urban examples of each from around the world. "Spaces of Retreat" tend to welcome the visitor into a realm removed from the chaos of the outside world. They usually advance a holistic approach to beauty, and the use of lower light levels and natural materials may characterize their designs. In many cases, they are located underground. "Spaces of Connection," on the other hand, capitalize on their proximity to the energy of the city beyond their doors. They may directly afford spectacular urban views, as with one lower Manhattan site. They often offer cultural amenities such as restaurants, cafés, Internet access, and, in one London barbershop, cinema fare. Some of these spaces are even welcoming guests without appointments for salon services or beauty treatments; that is to say, they are providing a place to grab a bite to eat, to check an email account, or to enjoy some all-around socializing.

The architects represented in these pages are some of the most gifted practitioners of their day, and these projects completed over the last five years have contributed to their ascendance in the design field. Tossing aside the standard assumptions about salon and spa design, clients have expanded traditional beauty programs in response to their patrons' desires, and architects have welcomed this impulse to challenge their formal vocabularies. The projects presented here vary tremendously in terms of size and budget; far from being a constraint, and perhaps surprisingly, the less lavish purses have spawned some of

I call beauty a social quality; for when men and women give us a sense of joy and pleasure in beholding them, they inspire us with sentiments of tenderness and affection towards their persons.

Edmund Burke,
Of the Sublime and Beautiful, 1812

the most creative solutions. Another "constraint" that has actually promoted some exceptional designs is the accommodation of the technical equipment required for the smooth operation of the facilities. The not infrequent choice to feature these mechanics in an open plan for all to see is one manifestation of "truthfulness." These architects have often transformed awkward, leftover spaces—typically former retail storage or dingy underground boxes. In one instance, the designers had to fit their scheme around a parking garage. A comprehensive understanding of these beauty programs on the part of their creators as intersections between the worlds of fashion, interior design, art, and architecture has led to unusually rich references as well as valuable collaborations. Consider the abstract, neon-toned photographic mural of enlarged hair follicles created by an artist for a Sydney hair salon. This site unwittingly recalls a distinguished history between art and beauty salons, specifically in the 1920s and 1930s, when Helena Rubinstein adorned her spaces with modernist sculpture and surrealist paintings to lend artistic legitimacy and sophistication to the mundane processes of perms and tints.

The designs featured here do not represent spaces of wellness devoted to a prolonged stay—each of the highlighted projects delivers beauty treatments in a single morning or afternoon. While the salon or spa offerings may have influenced the architects, no locations were selected for the particular treatments available, but rather for the careful sculpting of the spaces hosting these treatments. It also bears mentioning that while the projects have been separated as a means of commenting on parallel design forces—those of retreat and connection—which remain a valuable tool in a reading of today's beauty design market, two of the strongest works straddle this divide: Newly restored and expanded Georgian spa buildings in Bath, England, simultaneously connect visitors to a distinguished cultural history while providing a sense of escape from

present-day demands in a thoroughly modern setting; and a Los Angeles tanning salon invites us to temporarily isolate ourselves from the city, while its design celebrates a sense of place with a tribute to the surrounding billboards.

There's another movement afoot worth noting in spaces devoted to beauty: Leading department stores are featuring satellite locations of popular urban day spas, hoping to capitalize on the sale of their customized potions. For these retail vehicles (a London example is included here), architects are being asked to create scaled-down versions of their prototype designs, which are proving to be as signif-icant in the beauty branding equation as dis-tinctive product packaging. Finally, an emerg-ing category of contemporary spaces of beauty merits attention, although the designs have not yet caught up with the sophistication of the programs. What might be called "beauty in transit" speaks to the increasingly migratory patterns of our lives and evidences the recent trend toward primping on the fly. In airports from London to New York, Vancouver to Hong Kong, salons and spas are assisting travelers with their hectic schedules and extended lay-overs by maximizing down time on the ground. Unfortunately, the creators of these spaces are presently taking their design cues from mid-level hotel chains. If the evolution of the traditional beauty shop into the elegant and provocative spaces profiled here is any indica-tion, we may soon look forward to suffering air travel indignities in stylish spaces that at once respect and relieve the complexity of our lives.

SPACES OF RETREAT

In his lovely, resonant book *The Poetics of Space*, the phenomenologist Gaston Bachelard spoke of the intuitive affection we have for shells as demonstrating our need—from childhood through adulthood—for protection and security in a chaotic world: "an empty shell, like an empty nest, invites daydreams of refuge." No doubt he would have had a lot more to say of architecture's role in mediating the increasing complexity of our lives during the four decades since his death. But his simple evocation of the sense of safety provided by the image of the shell, in particular, is instructive for us to bear in mind as we review the salons and spas presented within Spaces of Retreat. Warm, dim, quiet, sheltered from view, and encouraging introspection, most of these places have much in common conceptually with Bachelard's model.

Not surprisingly, nature is an abiding force behind many of the designs. From river rocks in the floor of a New York spa treatment room to a pool in the private courtyard of a Los Angeles salon, natural forms and materials, even as abstractions, are employed to convey the idea of repose. Another model being advanced in the designs for these retreats is that of sacred architecture. This comparison arises in part from the ambiance created by designs that generally favor quiet over loudness, stillness over movement, and interior over exterior views. Water is a key element: visually and aurally it conveys the essence of purity—body and soul—that lives at the core of each form of worship. Consider that a Parisian perfumery whose entrance is marked by a large flower pond sells a product for children made from orange blossoms and honey called Baptismal Water.

Light, natural and otherwise, is especially significant in securing the appropriate sensibility for these calm spaces: Candles help to enhance the cavelike atmosphere of a subterranean meditation room in London; diffused light seeps between geometric cutouts in the walls of a Toronto day spa to draw attention to spaces that lie

beyond physical barriers; and hypnotic washes of green and blue tones produce a sense of serenity as they spill from the edges of a false ceiling in a salon near Boston.

When contrasted with the Spaces of Connection that follow, Spaces of Retreat are generally more contained, allowing for the privacy required by the various treatments offered. These interiors tend to be smaller and less open; they often invite clients to more secluded zones deeper within the space or below ground, as with a steam room in a Chicago mall site. Curves and corners are used to great advantage in creating a sense of obfuscation and to delineate separate spaces: A serpentine circulation pattern is articulated most dramatically with floor-to-ceiling fabric-swathed cabins in a New York skincare center, whereas acrylic cylinders at an English spa highlight the mysterious temporal nature of steaming water and its ability to veil a space.

Concerning the "daydreams of refuge" of which Bachelard spoke, unique natural forms can provide the mental space for retreat and even reverie. In their finest aspects, these man-made spaces take their cues from these forms and others like them, aspiring to and occasionally even achieving the same.

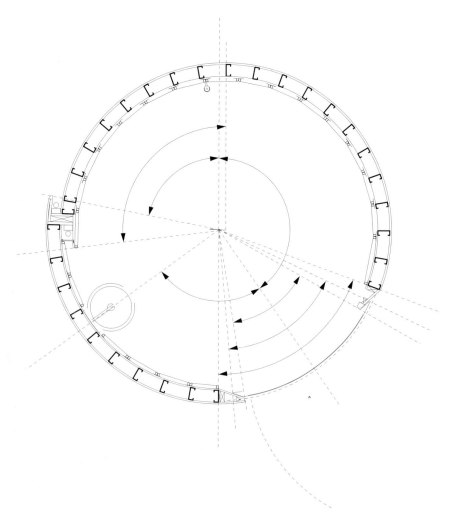

Cabin plan detail

Opposite: "The continuity of space and movement encourages exploration," explain the architects.

ARO (ARCHITECTURE RESEARCH OFFICE) WITH AOSHI KUDO

QIORA STORE AND SPA
NEW YORK

Qiora Store and Spa's dreamlike setting promotes ambiguity over legibility, making it a veritable albino zebra (the rarest sort) among retail venues. What is more, this ambiguity was announced through the vast windows of its location on New York's Madison Avenue—the world's most famous advertising center.

The fact that the spectacular space is already gone owing to the vagaries of the real estate market might suggest that the design was ahead of its time and renders the spa's environment even more elusive today.

For this project, the designers at ARO, led by Stephen Cassell and Adam Yarinsky, teamed up with Shiseido art director Aoshi Kudo to deliver the Japanese cosmetic company's skincare line to North America in one of the most elegantly sensual environments imaginable. From the street, the store appears like a stage set seen through a stark modernist composition of windows and glass entryway. Inside the 1,500-square-foot (139.5-square-meter), wedge-shaped space, multi-layered panels of blue organza stretch twenty feet from floor to ceiling. These curtained zones, roughly situated in the center of the floor plan, delineate three perfectly round private "cabins" where treatment beds reside. At either side of the entrance, products are displayed in blue glass bottles that seem to float on illuminated glass shelves. Lavatories and showers are aligned along the south wall toward the back. Interspersed throughout the store are waiting areas characterized by low curvaceous club chairs. Concealed from view, 12-foot (3.5-meter)-long fluorescent fixtures, dimmed and diffused by fabric, line the perimeter of the space. The remarkable lighting simulates daylight, modulating between warm and cool shades to make the skin glow; at night it adds to the sense of mystery in the other-worldly interior.

The deft melding of public and intimate space here is noteworthy. From the highly visible and crisp street façade, a snakelike circulation path around the cabins charts an aesthetic journey through an increasingly muted landscape to a realm of considerable visual silence. Arriving there we can't help but reflect on the very personal rewards of disengaging physically and psychically from the pace on the avenue outside the door to render ourselves fully present.

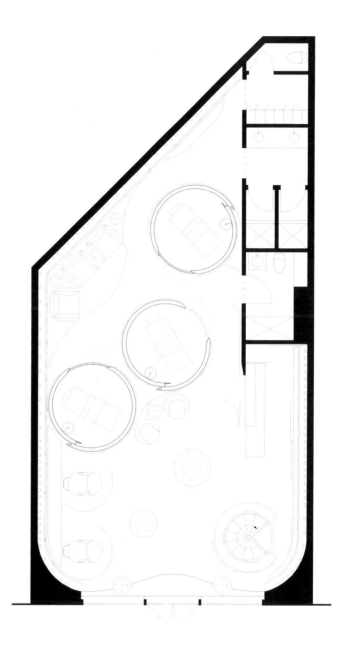

At night the store glows from
within and functions as a lantern
for passersby on Madison
Avenue.

Pristine white seating reflected in the clean, high-gloss white epoxy floors recalls the classic beauty of 1930s cinema sets.

Opposite: Feminine yet unfussy, the partially obscured display area waits to be activated by the presence of people. Custom fixtures are made of acrylic, glass, and stainless steel.

JACQUELINE AND HENRI BOIFFILS WITH FABIENNE CONTE-SEVIGNE AND FRANCIS GIACOBETTI

IUNX PARFUMERIE PARIS

The patented Ozmotek fragrance diffuser delivers the latest technology and is a sculptural element in its own right. Its glass bottles containing 25 milliliters (.8 fl oz) of fragrance are replaced regularly and last about four hundred hours.

Technological intervention and historical reference are beautifully married in the design for this Left Bank perfumery. The former trait is exploited in the unique method by which guests to the 3,330-square-foot (309.5-square-meter) boutique sample its more than sixty original fragrances: via an electric brushed aluminum diffuser that slowly releases a selected scent onto a card to "impregnate the space like a presence." Similar technology is employed to sample the aromas of lotions, shower gels, and room sprays. A summoning of the past finds equally poetic expression in both the development and description of the perfumery's offerings and in its architecture. Called into service by renowned perfumer Olivia Giacobetti are scents from our own pasts, such as marshmallow and smoldering embers, as well as fragrances extracted from medicinal plants first cultivated in the gardens of medieval monasteries. In Iunx (pronounced *yunks*), the design team of creative professionals—two architects, a makeup artist, and a photographer—sought to create a protective island where the fascination and seduction of aromas (the meaning of the store's ancient Greek name) and memory, both real and appropriated, intermingle.

A black-bottomed pond liberally populated with fresh floating flowers greets visitors at the entry and invites them to encounter the essence of the featured scents in their rawest form. This simple, elemental intervention speaks of sacred ritual and desire. The remainder of the dramatic amber-lit space, contained by canted walls like those of ancient Egyptian temple pylons, is devoted to olfactory discovery. The shopping experience here is meant to be an education; helping to achieve an atmosphere that is more gallery than retail space, the bulk of the products are hidden in full-height, smoked-glass-fronted display cases or stored within the thickness of the perimeter walls. The items on view appear to float out of the darkness like rare gems. In their desire to make fragrance become a "living language," the designers of Iunx have created nothing short of a visual haiku.

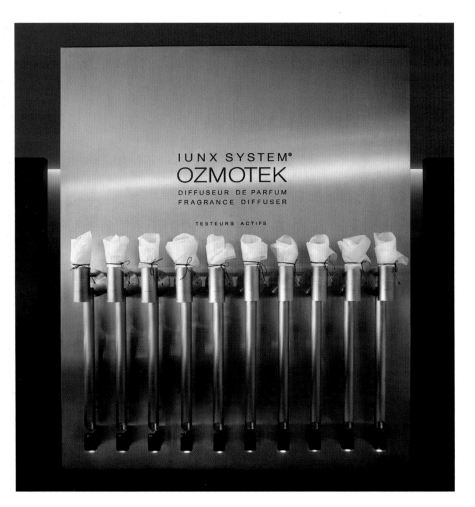

Opposite: Viewed from the entrance, a mammoth display cabinet containing the store's signature 300-milliliter (10 oz) flacons emerges from the pond and appears to be a column.

The display of scented waters in flacons reminds us of their scientific origins in a chemist's lab.

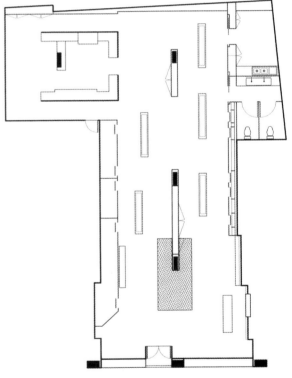

Candles and their corresponding scented tapers displayed before a beveled light well evoke a sense of mystery.

Opposite: Helping to characterize the cool atmosphere of the manicure stations are a metal beaded curtain and utilitarian desk lamps.

A portion of the reception area's wall voided at eye level encourages the first in a series of lingering gazes.

BURDIFILEK

CLEAR SPA & SALON TORONTO

"If you're getting your hair dyed, you don't want any surprises," says Paul Filek, explaining the importance of proper lighting in the refreshingly simple day spa he and his partner Diego Burdi designed in a residential section of northern Toronto. The duo specified fluorescents, which show colors accurately, for the manicure and hairstyling areas and halogens for the more meditative spa spaces. The effect is to create two distinct atmospheres of coolness and warmth.

Separating these two major sections of the 4,200-square-foot (390-square-meter) facility, a central multi-purpose lounge provides a place where guests can grab a bite or local professionals gather for meetings. And though the mood shifts from one end of the long space to the other, a consistent palette of materials—quarter-sawn ash veneer on plywood countertops, scratch-cut plaster walls, and a buff-colored epoxy-coated concrete floor—forges a strong aesthetic connection.

The designers have employed an additional means of visually integrating zones for various activities: in a creative maneuver that appeals to the voyeur in each of us, a series of carefully composed voids frame and control views throughout the space. For instance, in the central circulation corridor an absent vertical strip of wall might afford a glimpse of hands soaking in a manicure basin; another slot perfectly frames the terry-clothed figure of a spa guest sipping tea. These pictures are intentionally incomplete and likely to change in a moment, and are more beautiful, in fact, because of this ephemeral quality. The overall awareness of the proximity of others—and the inevitable question of when you yourself might be seen—never is invasive, but rather subtly sexy.

The ceiling plane is partially
dropped and specially lit over the
reception desk to assert the
orthogonal vocabulary of forms
that define the space.

In the public space of the lounge, softly draped curtains suggest but never reveal the daylight beyond, a measure that both connects and distances guests from the outside world.

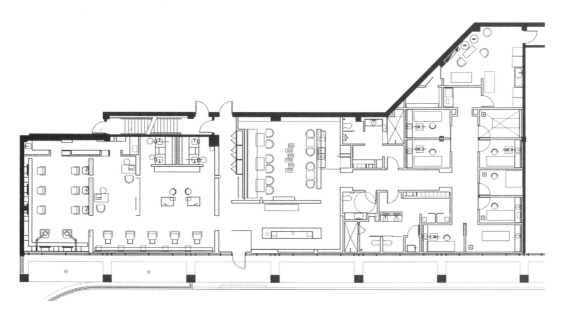

A repetitive motif of framing devices accomplished by cutouts in the walls of the manicure area creates a still-life composition of flowers in a vase.

The salon's haircutting zone features overhead spots to highlight and reveal true-to-life color.

A softly lit treatment room invites repose.

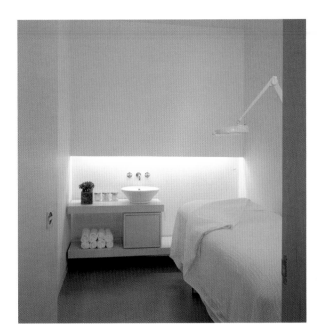

In a hallway leading to five treatment rooms, lights mounted in a dropped ceiling wash the walls with a muted glow.

The proportions of the ubiquitous mahogany wall boxes may be seen as echoing those of the entire long and narrow space of the spa.

Opposite: Sunset's purple glow washes over the traditional white storefront that is in keeping with the low profile of this downtown Manhattan block.

DESAI/CHIA STUDIO

PREMA NOLITA DAY SPA
NEW YORK

Long and narrow describes the typical floor plan in a New York apartment building, where storefronts occupy the street level and residences are stacked above like mounds of precut carrot sticks at the corner produce market. Such is the configuration of the tiny 600-square-foot (55.5-square-meter) Prema Nolita Day Spa, named for its lower Manhattan, "North of Little Italy" neighborhood.

The challenge for the architects, Arjun Desai and Kathy Chia, of Desai/Chia Studio, was to maintain the street's traditional scale yet to remedy the feeling of constraint, placing the focus instead on the healing products and practices within. Taking their cue from the contents of the all-natural lotions and ointments available for purchase, they specified only organic materials for the spa. The palette of mahogany, bamboo, slate, silk, and river rock results in a clean environment that nonetheless avoids being sterile. To this same end, the organic lines of the Eames chairs and George Nelson hanging lamps in the storefront offset the strong geometric angles of the other furnishings.

The designers left unconcealed a mysterious depression in the brick wall near the entrance, the trace perhaps of a fireplace. Everything else in this former coffee shop, from the furniture to the products, contributes to a highly crafted, rigorously composed space. Key to the spare concept is a series of long, narrow mahogany boxes, designed for product storage and hung slightly away from the walls on brackets to encourage the sense that they're floating inside the whitewashed shell.

The architects divided the spa into two main areas: in front, the retail section, which includes a "blending bar," comprises 400 square feet (37 square meters); a single treatment room and bath suite lie behind it and measure just 200 square feet (18.5 square meters). A pocket door may be drawn across the hall to separate the two functions formally. Beyond the private room, an unrealized garden space played a large role in informing the sense of repose that characterizes the project as a whole. A river rock "moat," visible along the edge of the floor of the treatment room, marks the threshold between indoors and out, where a piece of slate functions as a tiny bridge into what was intended as a post-treatment relaxation zone.

A remarkable attention to detail is evidenced in bamboo-clad hot water pipes and portable, Bento-inspired stacking trays that separate to offer functional surfaces at multiple levels.

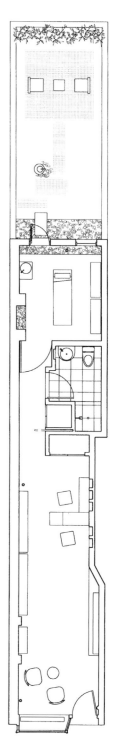

A mahogany "blending bar" divides the main room and serves as a consultation area for assisting clients in mixing essential oils into base formulas; it cleverly contains the cash wrap, too. Carved into the adjacent wall are square storage niches.

Despite its simplicity, guests in the treatment room have no doubt that their experience is custom-designed, from the bed of river rocks on the floor to the tall window that adds to the available light.

DMAC ARCHITECTURE

MARIO TRICOCI HAIR SALON & DAY SPA CHICAGO

When architect Dwayne MacEwen speaks of the "dislocation of the ground plane" in his subterranean design for the Mario Tricoci Hair Salon & Day Spa, he's referring to subtle gradations in the floor that signal various programmatic zones—something the body might pick up on before the eyes do. Through this kind of subtle design move, he promotes a larger sense of surprise in the city dwellers visiting this 17,000-square-foot (1,579.5-square-meter) space in a posh mall on Chicago's Miracle Mile; and it's a sensation intrinsic to its success. Drawing inspiration from medieval European streetscapes and ancient Turkish baths but employing materials with a modern sensibility, MacEwen's version

of an urban oasis is far from the leftover retail storage space the salon and spa once was.

Areas for salon activities are located adjacent to the entrance, while those for spa-related treatments require a journey deeper into the vast space. Spa guests have their own mezzanine-level manicure and cutting stations, located in a 4,000-square-foot (371.5-square-meter) loftlike area directly above the wet spaces. The largely open program needed to merge different requirements for patrons and technicians, so the architect designed custom furnishings, cabinetry, sinks, and light fixtures in order to incorporate typically "back of house" equipment into public spaces, thereby producing a consistent aesthetic. Strong visual axes transgress the physical separation of the two levels and provide an important dialogue between the spaces.

Materials such as Brazilian cherry, bamboo, limestone, back-painted and acid-etched glass, and stainless steel are typical enough of upscale contemporary interiors, but they're exploited here in creative ways. From the moment visitors descend by stairs or escalator from the mall into the double-height, 60-foot (18-meter)-long reception area, they feel the desired effect of immersion: Stainless steel inset banding separates planks of bamboo flooring in slowly graduated scales, suggesting a watery Doppler effect of progressively larger concentric circles tracing the passage of a sunken stone.

As guests enter the spaces of the spa, the palette becomes quieter. Advancing the idea of immersion is North America's first *hammám*. Above this humid spa anteroom a blue mosaic tile dome is pierced to allow for gentle illumination (fluorescent lamps are the true light source within this backlit oculus). Each spa activity room evolves from and is visually linked to this central space. For the walls and floors of the hydrotherapy rooms, MacEwen's approximation of a grotto ruin required the inexact matching of rough-cut limestone pieces laid in offset course, a technique resulting in soft shadows that sculpt an atmosphere as soothing as the treatments available here.

Opposite: A marriage of clean materials—Brazilian cherry wood, stainless steel, acid-etched glass—sets a modern tone in the reception area.

Clean-lined stainless steel product display cases situated next to a mirror and lit from below confer an authoritative, laboratory-like impression.

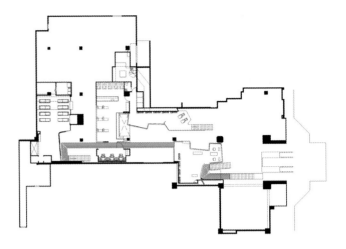

Plan of mezzanine level

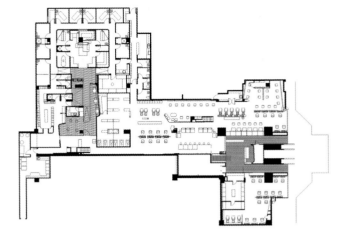

Plan of lower level

Modeled after similar spaces in ancient Turkish baths, the spa's *hammám* is centrally located and helps to gather and define the surrounding wet spaces.

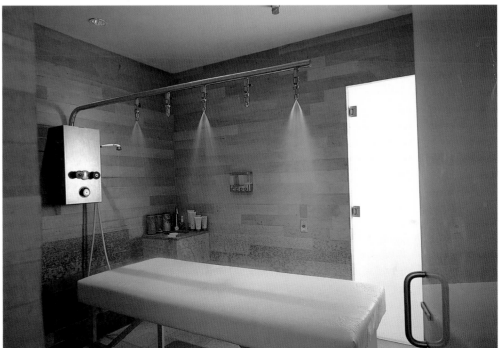

Shower misters hang like track lights over a bed in one of the spa's treatment rooms.

Opposite: Original body treatments such as the "Hay Detox and Pumpkin Facial" suggested the design of landscape elements that reference horticulture. Seen in the shampoo area and in the mezzanine above, bars of levitating wheatgrass characterize the space as much as any inorganic material.

A vertigo-inducing view from the outside entrance foreshadows the dreamlike interiors within Kenzo's new flagship location.

Opposite: Discard any preconceptions at the spa's door: Things are not what they appear from the moment one enters the biomorphic interior landscape.

EMMANUELLE DUPLAY

LABULLEKENZO PARIS

Cinematic art director Emmanuelle Duplay was perfectly cast in her role as the designer for Japanese fashion couturier Kenzo's new spa in Paris. This auspicious blurring of boundaries between artistic disciplines has yielded an exceptional collection of spaces. The spa is located on the Seine, across from the historic Pont Neuf bridge, in a wonderfully renovated six-story building whose exterior perfectly blends the art nouveau and art deco styles. The list of designers for spaces inside reads like a style magazine junkie's Who's Who: Apart from Kenzo's unparalleled clothing, there's a restaurant by Philippe Starck and one by Andrée Putman; Fabian Baron created the sparely beautiful perfume packaging that carries over seamlessly into Duplay's fourth-floor spa design.

In well under 2,000 square feet (186 square meters), Duplay has introduced a tangled bunch of themes that are somehow rendered harmonious. The space feels like an interior park where a series of architectural follies all open onto one another at once. There's the suspended hull-like form of ebony in the entry that introduces a wrapping motif that is repeated in other materials and at various scales throughout; it's a smart nod to the outside world of water, just paces past the door. Near the entrance, an enormous white molded form hangs midway between floor and ceiling, connected by cables, the lowermost ends of which disappear into the tallest fuchsia-colored shag rug imaginable. This display case looks as if it might elect to take off at any moment and therefore needs to be tethered. Shaped like an embracing set of arms, it contains, what else, "sensation tools" such as feather skin strokers. Everything culminates in the *bulles*, two treatment rooms that resemble nothing so much as giant marshmallows (the French translates as "bubble") the interiors of which offer vastly different atmospheres. The "sparkling" version, covered with synthetic fur, is lined inside with mosaic tiles and hung with a disco ball, while the "cocoon" version has a wide massage bed built directly into the dark wooden floor and soothing images projected onto the walls. From beneath and above, the rooms emanate yellow or violet light, respectively; in one of the designer's many playful gestures, the *bulles* appear to hover on illuminated carpets. This is an environment that seduces the senses, an enigmatic dreamworld clients can actually inhabit.

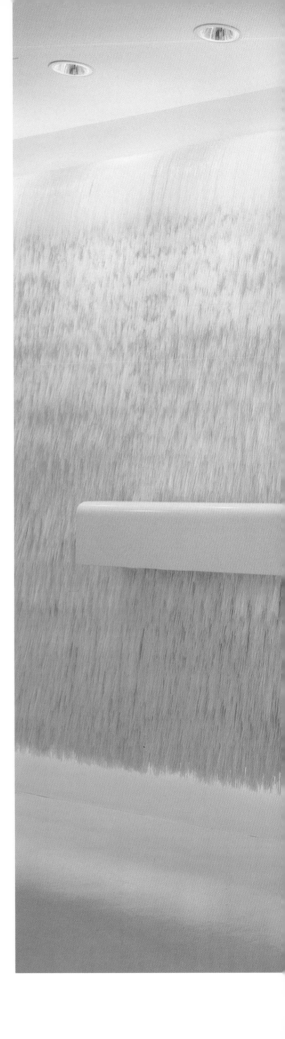

Opposite: The treatment rooms at the rear of the spa glow with light. Covered in synthetic hair from the roller brushes of a car wash, the *bulle* to the left blurs the boundaries between high and low art.

A loveseat in the skincare section exhibits the signature wrapped form featured elsewhere in the spa.

Floor, walls, and ceiling become
one in this seamless treatment
cave of golden iridescent
mosaic tile.

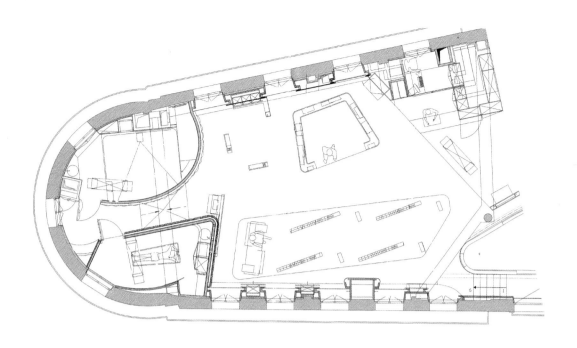

Peaceful images scroll slowly across the wall of a *bulle* and squares of changing light alter the ceiling above.

In pristine white display cases, a
red poppy from a perfume pack-
age is also trained to climb a wall.
Shifts in scale are selectively
employed throughout the space.

The spa's otherworldly hovering display case has museum-like quality and stature.

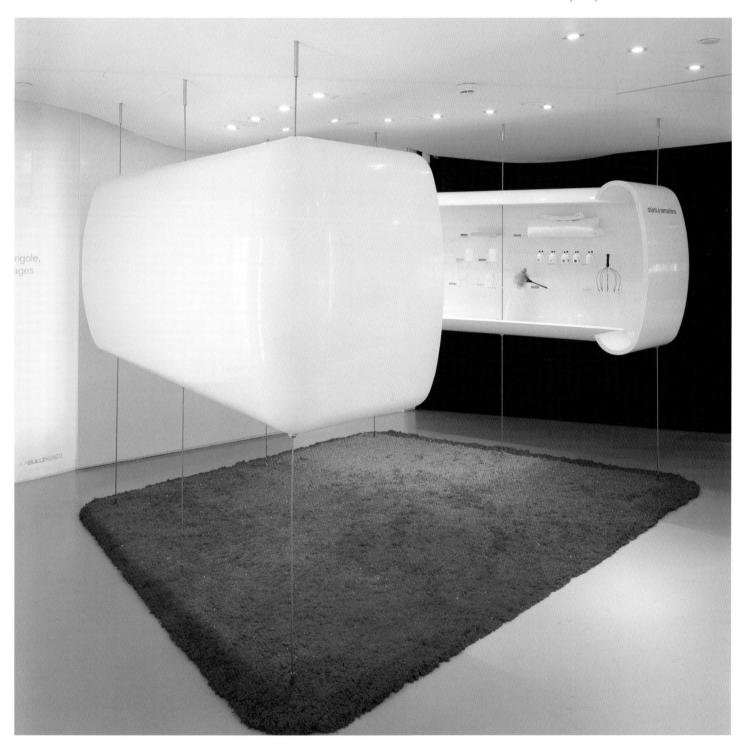

FUMITA DESIGN OFFICE

RYUKO HASSHIN HAIR SALON
TORIDE

Opposite: A precisely calculated intersection of material planes helps to weave together various functions in the salon's open floor plan.

A centrally positioned hinge allows the entry door to pivot in either direction and suggests an appealing narrative of comings and goings.

Akihito Fumita's coolly elegant hair salon, like its provincial locale northeast of Tokyo, a region known for surfing beaches and a robotics industry, strikes a perfect balance between boldness and studied restraint. It's a cucumber sandwich–like space of refinement, with a surprising kick of *wasabi* between its layers. A nearly monochromatic color palette (there are russet-toned chairs in the waiting area) and minimal materials exemplify the overall sense of reduction in the small, 1,227-square-foot (114-square-meter) beauty shop. Typical of the fastidious design detail throughout is the sweeping curve of its generously proportioned glass façade leading guests to what appears to be a partially opened door; this slight skewing of the entry combined with recessed lighting acts as a provocative invitation to passersby.

Another illusory move has produced perhaps the loveliest aspect of the clients' experience here: At the spare styling stations, silvering applied to the inner side of a series of pristine glass boxes opposite the chairs functions as mirrors and produces a gallery of floating portraits. The glass box is reiterated in a horizontal orientation as a shelving unit suspended nearby. In an environment this open every gesture, large, small, and even those unseen, is significant. Echoing the macaroni-shaped lights suspended overhead is an illuminated counter's edge leading to the cashier's desk, a seemingly disembodied fluorescent streak drawn across the room like the horizon line in a painting. Less dramatic but supremely functional are the metal recesses built into the salon's circular glass-topped tables that contain handles so that the furniture may be moved without marring its surface. Reflective surfaces such as the gleaming white resin floor and stainless steel built-ins contribute to maximizing the sense of space.

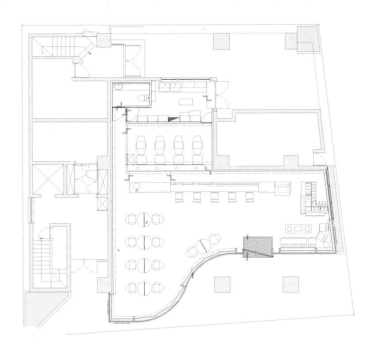

Opposite: The pristine environment that lies beyond the salon's curving glass wall, although entirely visible from the street, conveys a hushed sense of remove, as if in a diorama.

Dutch De Stijl master Gerrit Rietveld would recognize his architectonic influence in this planar construct that contains the cash wrap in a stainless steel cubic volume.

GRIMSHAW

THERMAE BATH SPA BATH

Imagine bathing and relaxing with beauty treatments in warm water that fell as rain thousands of years ago. Add a setting evocative of a James Bond film from the Roger Moore era and you could well be in the new steam room of the Thermae Bath Spa. With mushrooming concrete columns rising from private pools secured in cylindrical acrylic tanks, and reflected daylight painting the bodies of fellow bathers in diffused light and shadow, it's a biomorphic wet dream of a space.

When Britain's Millennium Commission wisely saw fit to reinvest in some of the nation's leading architectural treasures, the structures housing the country's only naturally occurring thermal hot springs, in Bath, fit the bill perfectly. The restoration of two stone spa buildings dating from the 1770s and the design of the new modern facility was entrusted to the architectural firm of Sir Nicholas Grimshaw after its striking scheme linking old and new structures triumphed in a fierce competition. Overall, the nearly £8 million ($15 million) grant provided the foundation for the project's 39,000-square-foot (3,623-square-meter) reconfiguration.

One of the most valuable aspects of the renovation and addition is its success in opening up vistas among new, old, and ancient spaces, forging a visual connection between wildly disparate eras. From a new rooftop pool, visitors experience a layering of images and, by extension, time: framed by glass panels, views encompass a landscape replete with Gothic church spires and Roman ruins. Interior juxtapositions within the recently joined spaces are equally dramatic and thought provoking. Happily, this is a case where savvy cultural preservation has resulted in a harmonious cultural creation befitting its own age.

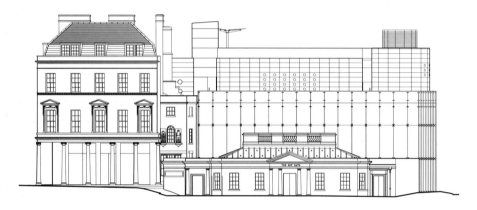

West elevation

Opposite: As evening descends on an ancient street, the provocative glow of the new spa beckons.

Following page: The mushroom columns in the steam room recall Frank Lloyd Wright's interiors for the Johnson Wax headquarters.

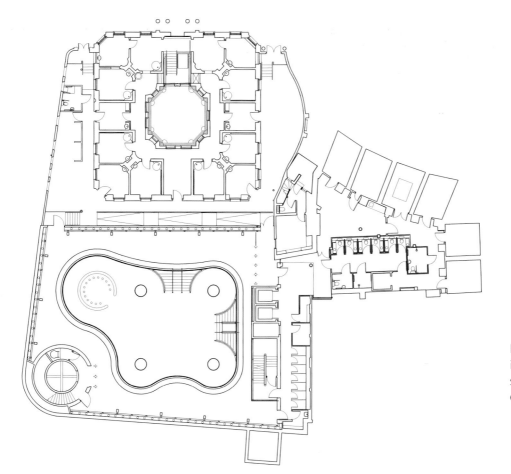

Plan of lower ground level, showing the circular forms of the main spa pool in contrast to the rectilinear forms of the treatment rooms

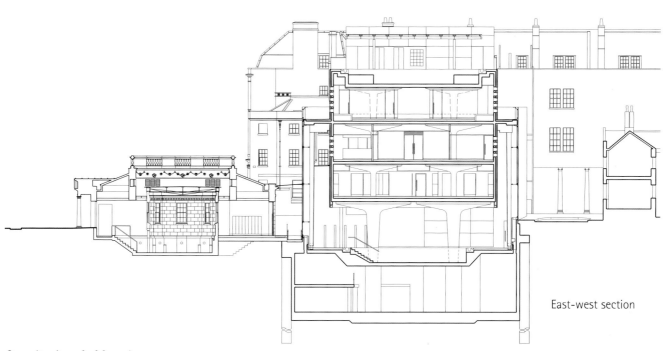

East-west section

Opposite: A roof of frameless glass panels—one of the knighted architect's hallmarks—encloses the Hot Bath, an eighteenth-century space that recalls the baths of Roman emperors.

The cabana for the rooftop pool boasts a repetitive fin motif that echoes the series of chimneys in an adjacent structure. Bath Abbey soars in the background.

At Calmia Day Spa the prevalent motif of leaves is abstracted in a decorative gesture for the lower-level spa corridor.

GROVES NATCHEVA ARCHITECTS

CALMIA DAY SPA AND CALMIA AT SELFRIDGES LONDON

At Calmia Day Spa, on London's sophisticated Marylebone High Street, a ground-floor half level links two floors offering distinctly different services and atmospheres. Up top is the retail component, which may be viewed from the street through enormous plate-glass windows. Here clothes, books, and treatment products are displayed amidst a sculptural landscape designed as an urban abstraction of nature. A second interior stairway provides passage down to a hidden spa realm with four treatment rooms and a relaxation suite. This subterranean space takes its inspiration from the Tibetan prayer halls and Balinese resorts visited by the owner, a style editor for *The Times,* on her extensive travels.

Architects Murray Groves and Adriana Natcheva were commissioned to develop an architectural language that would embody the Calmia brand, and their colorful, modernist vocabulary has since been translated for another, smaller retail venue within Selfridges department store. The design for the flagship West End spa had to contend with an awkward triangular floor plate that accommodates an underground parking lot. This inherited constraint finds powerful, if subliminal, expression in the labyrinthine construction of the product display area—a design now curiously characteristic of both sites. Common to the two locales are cool, luminous retail zones with sandlike surfaces augmented by troughs of water upon which float clusters of flowers. A dark resin floor inlaid with water lilies leads to changing rooms at the store and to the treatment area at the spa; in each case, an explosion of brilliant tropical colors muted by lower lighting announces the transitions.

The wraparound planar construction for displaying items at the flagship spa—shown empty here—was made of MDF and coated with a waterproof sand and resin mixture normally found on hospital and factory floors.

A treatment room at the original
Calmia offers the ultimate repose.

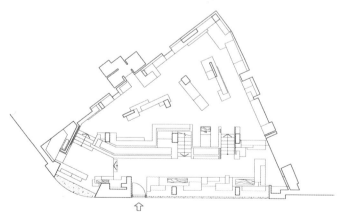

Plan of the ground level of
Calmia Day Spa

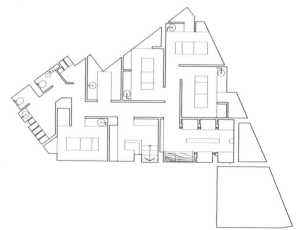

Plan of the lower ground level

The candlelit communal relaxation suite at the West End location, based on a Tibetan prayer hall, exudes an appropriate sense of hermetic detachment.

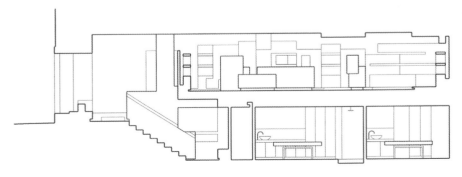

Section of Calmia Day Spa

The tea bar and till station at
Selfridges offers a place to rest
and prepare oneself before re-
entering the outside world.

Also at Selfridges, a consultation
table of jigsaw-seeming construction hovers over the signature
resin floor inlaid with lily pads.

The entry to the changing area at Selfridges is a bold declaration of the thematic abstraction of nature that characterizes these ultra-urban spaces.

Highly lacquered surfaces in the Selfridges changing rooms reflect their surroundings to maximize the small space.

MOLNAR FREEMAN ARCHITECTS

WINK! HAIR SALON
SYDNEY

A major structural obstacle in the plan for this Sydney hair salon gave rise to its most innovative aspect. A solid masonry stairwell in the center of the 1,076-square-foot (100-square-meter) space necessitated a literal turnaround in design direction; consequently, Wink! now lays claim to a surprisingly efficient dogleg-shaped interior. With the help of digital artist James McGrath, architect Katie Molnar turned lemons into first-rate lemonade.

Taking her cue from the curved wall of the stair, Molnar inscribed a larger corresponding arc several yards distant to delineate the parameters of the salon's public space. Washrooms and storage occupy the leftover segment, out of view. She then altered the physical character of the opaque, impermeable stair wall by specifying a mural to wrap around the curve; it acts to dematerialize the solid form. A vinyl digital image is sandwiched between two acrylic panels, behind which are located fluorescent battens. The sleight-of-hand operation results from the illuminated design's ability to suggest depth and transparency where none exist. The colorful abstracted lines of the mural were chosen on the theory that they might provide greater food for thought than prevalent glossy magazine fare. They also happen to be most appropriate in this application: McGrath enlarged hair follicles from medical journals and wire-framed them using computer modeling.

The prominent curve of the stairwell is highlighted again where it meets the strict grid of the black tile floor, which reflects the symphony of lights above. The rounded form also inspired the selection of white acrylic chairs that resemble manta rays in motion. In these and other regards, the overall space communicates the sense of being underwater: the filtered, reflected, and wavering views remind us of the Australian coastal city the salon calls home.

Mirrors on the opposite wall further fragment the graphics on the paneled mural at the center of the space.

Hair washing stations line the newly created curved wall opposite the belly of the stairwell.

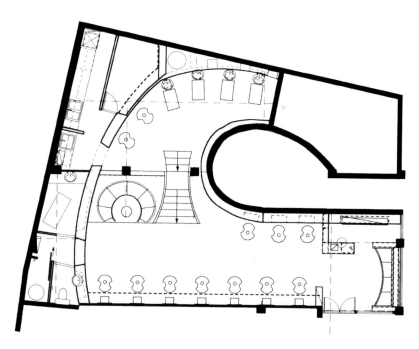

The clear plastic joiners that divide the digital panels of the mural double as vertical light sources that send radiating patterns onto the ceiling.

their favorite stars. Enter Mehran Shahverdi, who designed the environment of relaxed luxury that promotes the sense that everything is possible—the invaluable intangible that has long drawn so many to the City of Angels.

The U-shaped salon sits in a 3,000-square-foot (279-square-meter) space in West Hollywood that once housed offices for Neil Diamond. At its center a courtyard surrounds a deep pool. One side is configured as an open salon and the other is divided into two intimate styling zones. While these areas may be viewed from one another through layers of glass, a private room with a secret entrance caters to celebrities. In good feng shui form, a granite fireplace in the reception area balances the outdoor water element. Each of the sixteen stations (a number that is kept purposefully small) is equipped with a video recorder so that clients can review sessions at home. Twelve-foot Douglas fir counters, nickel-plated mirror frames, and floor-to-ceiling glass windows contribute to the clean, modern interiors. Narrow slots cut in the roof above the styling stations provide additional light and reinforce the indoor/outdoor connection throughout. Elsewhere, a dropped ceiling accommodates a newly installed HVAC system for optimal ventilation.

These quantifiable details, however, don't convey the uniqueness of the space. Instead, the experience may perhaps best be understood in terms of individual moments that reflect the remarkable quality of L.A.'s indoor/outdoor lifestyle, exploited here to its fullest: entering the ivy-covered enclave through tall, antique Egyptian doors that lead to a sky-lit passageway straight from the French Quarter; sitting poolside, cappuccino in hand, contemplating a fallen bougainvillea blossom as it rides the water currents in a faint February breeze—the magenta flower the color of the saturated walls in the entrance hall. Subtle details such as these amount to a serene, sophisticated environment designed for well-being, one ironically in which the importance of star power recedes into the background.

The dramatic entry, with its magenta walls and delicate wrought-iron details, is on axis with the mirrored-glass wall that terminates the courtyard pool.

Opposite: This quintessential portrait of Los Angeles's indoor/outdoor lifestyle nicely equates natural beauty with the more studied version within.

MSH DESIGN

SALLY HERSHBERGER AT JOHN FRIEDA LOS ANGELES

At $400 (£215) per haircut and with a months-long waiting list, stylist Sally Hershberger is clearly offering more than the typical salon experience. She's often creating a whole new look: the debut of Jane Fonda's shag cut at the Oscars a few years back; a collaboration with Tom Cruise on the perfect ponytail for his sleazy, mold-breaking *Magnolia* character. She's made over the tresses of Meg Ryan, Courtney Love, Michelle Pfeiffer, Ed Norton, and Nicole Kidman. Of course, more than a fair share of her clientele are paying to achieve the carefree look of

Sliding glass doors, usually left open, are all that separate the entry area from the courtyard.

Viewed from a styling station, the spare geometric lines of the pergola serve in contrast to the lush and serpentine organic material.

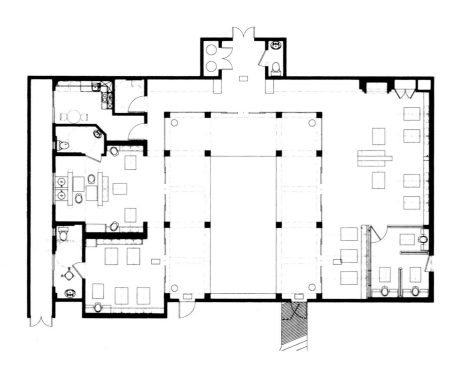

Yellow vertical light strips along either side of the mirrors leap out from a distance and recall Dan Flavin's light sculptures.

Opposite: The mirrored wall reflects back the beautiful symmetry of the poolside setting.

OFFICE DA

JOLI HAIR DESIGN
CHESTNUT HILL

Pragmatic and poetic purposes are neatly aligned in this cleanly executed, 1,600-square-foot (148.5-square-meter) salon offering health and beauty treatments on two levels. Located among other street-front shops in a vital urban community at Boston's western edge, Joli whispers more than it shouts. Even large-scale design gestures such as a tremendous floating ceiling that hovers over the hair, manicure, and pedicure services on the ground floor help to define rather than overwhelm the space. And because the suspended plaster form conceals mechanical systems, there's nothing extraneous in the sparely appointed room. Along a wall opposite the reception area open product display cases made of dark wood sit atop stark white storage cabinets; the blocks of saturated colors provided by the packaging lend a crisp accent that contrasts nicely with the ubiquitous soft green light washing the walls above.

Clients desiring spa treatments descend to the private massage and skincare facilities below via a simply composed, centrally located stairway lined with a plywood sleeve. On this dimly lit level, fabric is used to divide spaces visually and acoustically. Round sconces pop through highly textured mouthlike openings in the slashed charcoal-colored felt that insulates the walls. With unusual moves like this, Monica Ponce de Leon and Nader Tehrani of Office dA have clearly taken aesthetic chances—and have succeeded in challenging our notions of materiality as well as what constitutes appropriate salon architecture. That such an intimate interior space can so easily house a monumental sculptural form more readily found at freeway overpasses is remarkable testament to the team's unbridled vision.

Opposite: A lovely play of symmetry occurs in the echo of the ceiling and stairwell forms.

Thin brass posts, typical of the refined materials chosen throughout, mark the rear of the salon.

The ceiling appears to emerge from the back wall like an organic growth, bringing to mind Eero Saarinen's sculptural concrete forms.

Opposite: Bathed in colored light, the plaster walls and ceiling meet in a highly abstract composition.

The heavy felt that lines the walls of the lower level is slit to reveal integrated light sources.

Opposite page: Seen from below, the strict geometry of the plywood-lined stairs channels our view together with our thoughts upward and toward the out-of-doors.

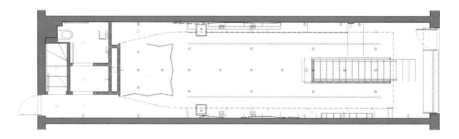

Plan of ground level

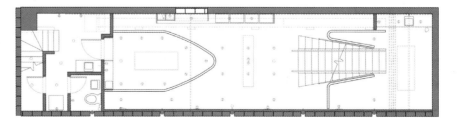

Plan of lower level

REFLECTING BEAUTY

Spaces devoted to beauty treatments offer plenty of pragmatic reasons to use reflective surfaces, starting with "verification and vanity," as Nader Tehrani of Office dA puts it. Mirrors facilitate the desire of clients to check the progress of a cut, color, or wax job and provide for a face-to-face conversation with the technician standing beside or behind them. The doubling exercise practiced by mirrors also increases available light and the perceived depth of space within a room, benefits achieved at a comparatively small material expense. In the design Tehrani and partner Monica Ponce de Leon devised for the James Joseph Salon in Boston, the team elevated the concept of reflection to a primary role. Owing to a scant budget, explains Tehrani, "the intellectual economy of the mirror offered the only real freedom to design."

In their project, the idea of mirrors acting as windows is exploited to its fullest potential and given expression in two distinctly different ways: The only natural light entering the second-story space issues from windows along the street wall. The desire to maximize the number of styling stations, however, suggested the need for a partition in this area that would support mirrors on either side—thereby cutting off the light source for half the stations and the remainder of the space. Office dA fulfilled both economic and aesthetic concerns by suspending a series of back-to-back blade mirrors from mountain climbing cables anchored in the ceiling. As a result, additional light comes flooding through. Moreover, in size, the mirrors mimic the room's real apertures so they function as trompe-l'oeil windows, bringing in scenes from the outdoors and creating surreal moments worthy of Magritte. As a bonus, the mirrors signal to passersby below who might not otherwise be aware of the salon's location.

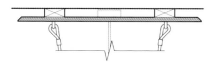

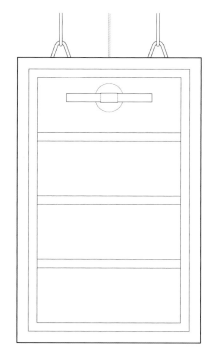

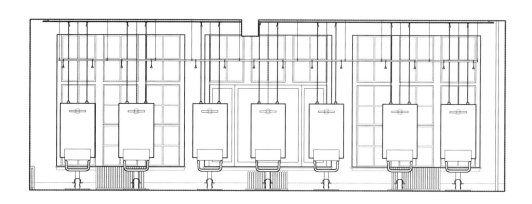

Tehrani likens this mirror application to introducing a second set of punched windows; the team's other sophisticated take on reflection in the salon replicates the composition of ribbon windows. Framed alternating frosted and mirrored glass ensembles hang along the length of an interior brick wall in a horizontal orientation. Behind the frosted glass fluorescent lamps supply the light that contributes to realizing the illusion of the windows after which they are modeled. Rather than offering a panoramic view to the outdoors, however, here expectations are undermined to produce an alternative bounty—the sense of yet more interior space and oblique views of the suspended reflections nearby.

As Tehrani suggests, the intellectual economy of mirrors can be liberating. Reflection places value on repetition and symmetry; it can introduce the concept of order and infinity into tightly contained spaces. A mirror also helps to identify spectacles, directing the gaze to particular vignettes, calling out and framing spaces within a space. The power of reflection to transport us is enduring. It transcends physical boundaries, giving access to realms not accessible to our bodies.

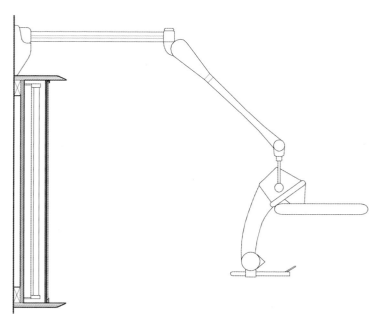

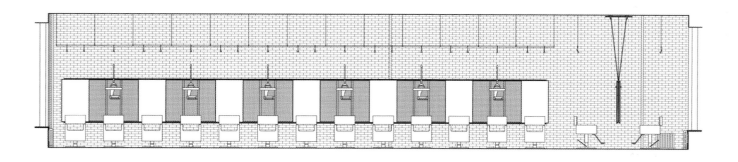

Mirrored glass isn't the only material performing these operations: Reflections produced by water also provide an opportunity to see the world, however fleetingly, in a different light. The Irish architect Clodagh employs water as a primary material element in her spa building for the Kiawah Island Club in South Carolina. By locating an infinity pool at the entrance—the portal to a body beautiful experience—she invites guests to take leave of their bodies for a moment and meditate instead on things larger than themselves: the roundness and smoothness of the river rocks that line the shallow pool, the expansiveness of the sky. Here, reflection operates on a metaphorical level and as a means of connecting to the surrounding marshlands and to the horizon beyond, a reminder that everything is part of the same continuum. This design gesture appears once again inside the spa, where a hallway terminates at a reflecting pool flanked by a concrete bench. The repetition of the watery reflection challenges the visitor's sense of orientation by transferring a scene from outside onto the floor within. The more intimate scale encourages guests to dip a hand into the pool, and to disturb the image floating on its surface in order to reconcile what they see with what they thought they knew.

The currency of reflection in these programs is evidenced altogether differently by the building that houses Lumière Salon in Providence, Rhode Island (profiled in the following section). "We're interested in having architecture act as an instrument that creates phenomena," says Kyna Leski of 3SIX0. With the aid of 8,000 reflective copper rods, Leski and her partner Christopher Bardt transformed the ground-floor space of a derelict old building with good bones into one of the city's finest new spaces. And from the exterior, during the day, it's the face of the city that is showcased in the reflections from the floor-to-ceiling rods hanging in the salon's expansive windows. Leski sees the intervention, which from a passerby's perspective amounts to strands of the rounded reflective material alternating with the flat clear glass of the window, as a screen that "places your eye." Part of its visual appeal is the apparent dematerialization of the projected buildings across the street. When the air conditioning is turned on or someone introduces a breeze into the salon by opening the door, the rods reassemble themselves, as does the image. It's a subtle, nuanced rendition of the inconstant doubling of Venetian architecture by that city's ubiquitous canals, a thoroughly delightful encounter made possible by designers for whom the simple laws of physics prove irresistible. Perhaps this is the greatest benefit of using reflection to define a space: inducing wonder. Reflection, above all, suggests that there is always more.

SPACES OF CONNECTION

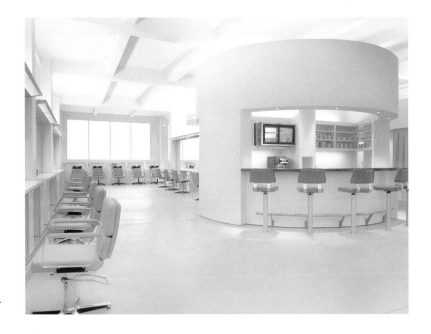

The ability of design to reflect (and on occasion even anticipate) sociological and cultural changes makes it a valuable tool for understanding contemporary life. The spaces gathered here demonstrate our desire to reach out to one another and share experiences; unsurprisingly, a primary goal in the designs for each is cultivating an atmosphere of exchange. The types of connections made possible are as diverse as the designs featured: from the social connection exemplified by an intergenerational gathering in the garden of an Upper East Side salon to a technological connection in a north of Detroit salon, where passersby on the sidewalk are privy to live video feeds of the styling techniques being employed beyond the glass façade. By contrast with the Spaces of Retreat, these venues stress stimulation over security and drama over dharma.

Whether they're offering a physical or a virtual connection, Spaces of Connection are about seeing and being seen. In San Francisco a salon regularly holds fashion shows in a dramatic space that doubles as a café where visitors are perpetually on display. In a Soho salon clients make an entrance along a stairway fashioned like a runway and while they check in at the reception desk, their image is broadcast on the company's website. And at the forefront of a growing trend, the salon provides customers with the technology to surf the Web or check their email while they await their appointments.

In two prominent salon examples, the venues are intimately scaled: A party atmosphere is advanced in a clubby London barbershop where male clients compete at GameBoy and Playstation, and young women exchange gossip over pedicures at Dublin's first nail bar. Both spaces exploit materials that are sleek, sexy, and meant to communicate fun—a sinuous fuchsia velvet wall in the latter and fiberglass swing-out sinks in the former.

More often, though, these spaces are large and light with open sightlines or may be designed to draw attention to particular views in

an effort to mine the context of their existing sites for whatever bounties they may offer. They subscribe to the philosophy that an expansive space can help one to feel more expansive inside, a doctrine perhaps made most evident in the places that welcome the city into their interiors. In the most stunning example of this exercise, an eighth-floor reception lounge with panoramic views of downtown Manhattan has become a prime location for neighborhood folks to meet over tea or coffee—with every hair already perfectly in place. Passersby figure into the designs of hair and skin salons in Montréal and Santa Monica as essential background flavor, significant aesthetic and cultural elements in ever-changing urban tableaux just beyond the windows. The design for a Los Angeles tanning salon was actually inspired by the surrounding billboards, playing up rather than overlooking an immediate connection to its generic mini-mall site.

Architecture is foremost a social activity, a collaboration in the truest sense. These spaces in particular rely on the interdependence of a number of elements for their success, but mostly they require the presence of people to become activated. There's a sense that their guests are contributing to some kind of spectacle, and by the time they leave, ideally a bit transformed in both body and mind, they carry that energy out into the world where it attracts even more.

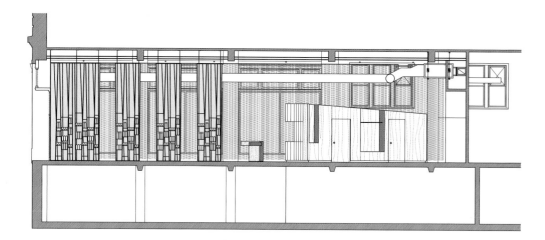

Section

Opposite page: A cherry and glass wall screen displaying products in the entry and reception area separates incoming guests from those well into their primping.

3SIXO

LUMIÈRE SALON PROVIDENCE

Lumière Salon's radiant interior in the Providence, Rhode Island, neighborhood called Downcity has mythical appeal, inspiring wonder and cultivating the imagination as it glows like a barely contained fire. Lesser architects would have generated a far more literal interpretation of the clients' desire that a crown be part of the branding image for their new hairstyling enterprise. But 3SIXO's principals, Christopher Bardt and Kyna Leski, reviewed the 1,850 square-foot (172 square-meter) program's practical and fantastical aspects together, without losing sight of opportunities for original expression. And rather than altering the character of the generously proportioned old space, they exploited its virtues.

The highly visible corner site boasted sizable adjacent glass elevations—an appropriate expression of the building's historicism, but not exactly affording privacy for the activities within. The design team's solution was to create a sophisticated scrim using 8,000 copper rods that hang from the 17-foot (5-meter) ceilings down to the floor. During the salon's operating hours, due to the wealth of daylight outside, clients have full vantage of the city beyond the windows, but are protected from the view of passersby, who instead glimpse themselves and their surroundings in the reflective copper and plate glass. As darkness falls at closing time, the scenario reverses, offering the city an enchanting spectacle of the salon's brilliantly lit interior.

Beginning with the rods at the perimeter and taking in an elaborate cherry and glass product display screen and a series of diagonally placed cutting stations, the progressive layering of interior elements within the space was inspired by the increasingly intimate effect of moving deeper into a forest. The journey culminates at the back wall, where folds of fabric shape manicure and pedicure alcoves; the material both baffles sound and softens the space. Toward the rear, a large freestanding cherry wedge houses the changing room and lavatory. A 70-foot (21.5-meter)-long mirror wall, thickened to contain a hair coloring lab, hair dryers, and storage closets, extends the length of the catwalk and offers the beautiful space back to itself.

"Life on the street is included in the experience of the salon, and the salon ritual is part of the life of the city," note the architects.

The mirror wall, seen here looking toward the back of the salon, is etched to allow rays of light from behind to project through.

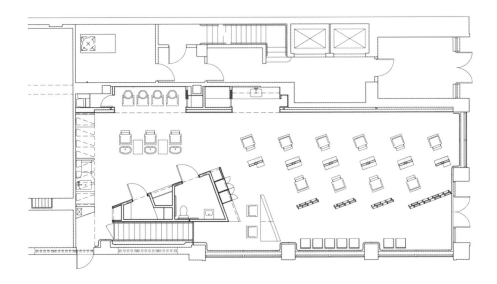

An abundance of reflective surfaces in a view facing the street intensifies the salon's lighting scheme.

A row of diagonally positioned cutting stations in stainless steel features double-sided mirrors.

Opposite: A window detail frames the dramatically luminous interior in an abstract light composition.

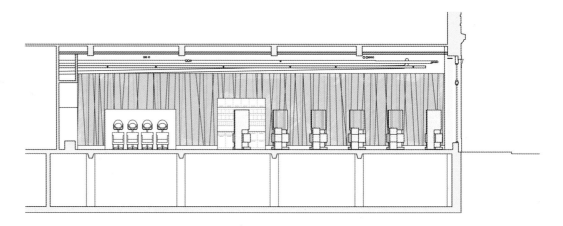

Section

ABRAMSON TEIGER ARCHITECTS

DERMALOGICA ON MONTANA
SANTA MONICA

The design for this flagship skin care center and store in one of L.A.'s toniest beachside communities was inspired by ideas about contrast and juxtaposition. Operating on both macro and micro levels, these themes unfold in a circulation narrative that leads from an exposed streetscape into the sensory isolation of three treatment "pods;" en route through the 1,662-square-foot (154.5-square-meter) space, guests experience an unusual play of materials, textures, and forms meant to enhance one another via their differences.

In the smooth, shiny surface of the white undulating pods, architects Trevor Abramson and Douglas Teiger articulate a spatial analogy to "the malleable nature of skin," as Abramson puts it. Existing columns that couldn't be moved determined their locations, and to balance the visual weight of the pods, the main wall opposite, behind the cashiers, is constructed of highly textured, beige brick, laid without mortar. A long and sleek white Corian counter delineating this area sits atop a wide-planked, dark wood base. Colors from the packaging of skin care products, neatly displayed on the entry wall, reappear as accents elsewhere in the small facility, such as the green, blue, and orange tones strewn like confetti on skinny columns.

To catch the attention of pedestrians in this dense shopping zone, the architects installed an 8 × 8-foot (2.5 × 2.5-meter) sliding pocket window on the Montana Avenue side of the new corner doorway. In the light and open reception area and skin bar they have created an engaging social environment where people can play with products. From the spa's entrance, the highly glossed concrete floor rakes downward slightly drawing visitors deeper into the space.

Apart from the altered entrance, the Spanish-style building dating from 1926 resembles its neighbors—until nighttime, that is, when from within the dark recesses of the treatment rooms, a psychedelic light emanates from each stark white pod, transforming the interior into a black-light fantasy.

The malleable and glowing qualities of healthy skin inspired the forms and surfaces of three shiny treatment pods.

Opposite: This perspective takes in the "body" of the store, as experienced looking from the back of the spa toward the entry passage.

Materials such as Corian and brick in the reception area contrast with those of the slick, biomorphic pods, constructed of marble dust and stucco–coated dry wall over curved metal frames.

Opposite: Dermalogica's Montana Avenue façade welcomes Santa Monica shoppers with an expansive view of the interior.

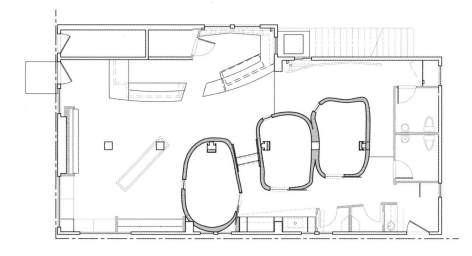

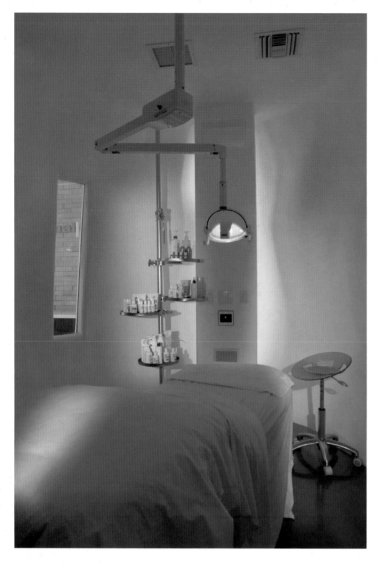

Inside the treatment pods, a single panel allows aestheticians to vary the mood by controlling lighting, sound, and temperature. Supplies and products hang from a treatment "tree."

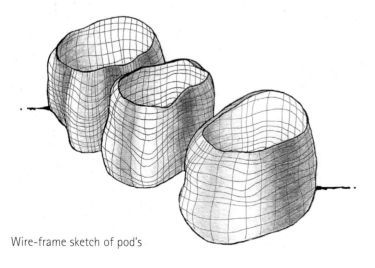

Wire-frame sketch of pod's

Electrified windows in the pods, opaque during daytime client sessions, become clear at night, conveying blue light from within.

Ever present in the salon's design, the city may be glimpsed as one descends the stairway.

Opposite: A wooden catwalk in the reception/café area does double duty as a runway for hair and fashion shows or as a bench for patrons not seated at the window bar.

ANDERSON ARCHITECTS WITH SELLDORF ARCHITECTS

BUMBLE AND BUMBLE.SALON
NEW YORK

From the home of hardcore sex clubs in the early 1980s to the site of *Sex and the City* scenes two decades later, Manhattan's Meatpacking District has witnessed some significant changes. Over the past few years some of New York's nattiest clothing boutiques have been located in the area. The newest neighbor in the fashionista crowd is Bumble and bumble.Salon, the downtown outpost of the hairdressers to myriad magazine cover girls. Along with a hipper address,

the renowned salon has initiated a revolutionary concept in its new design: Instead of gazing at themselves during their consultations and coifs, clients engage lofty northern and southern views of Manhattan and its environs—a vista that moves from midtown skyscrapers to sweep across the lower Hudson River, taking in the Statue of Liberty, Ellis Island, and Jersey City. Mirrors on rollers are available for quick peeks if clients so desire; however, their absence is already improving communication between clients and stylists.

The project specified that an existing warehouse of three stories be renovated and five additional floors added. Selldorf Architects did the exterior work and anderson architects the interiors. Bumble occupies six floors: The fourth and fifth floors accommodate offices; the third and sixth floors house an auditorium and classrooms for Bumble and bumble.University, which offers intensive training for stylists worldwide. The seventh floor is devoted to cutting, coloring, and styling and the eighth serves as a reception lounge and café. Linking the upper floors are two trim white metal staircases, which provide great overall views of the proceedings.

The 40,000-square-foot (3,716-square-meter) salon is rough and ready in appearance and artful in its lack of self-consciousness. The color palette is clean and subdued; materials are simple, durable, and environmentally responsible: concrete floors and walls of Plysum (typically used as an insulating panel) or painted sheetrock with plywood veneers. Medium-density fiberboard delineates the changing rooms, which feature grey industrial felt cut to recall the refrigeration strips in neighboring meatpacking facilities. A flood of daylight helps to orient clients. Above all, there's a constant energy here that replicates that of its surroundings; indeed, the Bumble enclave has been referred to as a self-contained village of sorts. New Yorkers often visit the top-floor lounge specifically to eat a sandwich, check email, or hold a business meeting while soaking in the striking views and connecting to their city below.

While transformations take place in this seventh-floor cutting and styling area, the city provides an ever-changing barometer of its own.

Plan of seventh floor

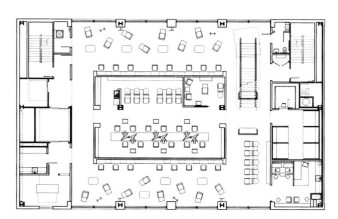

A repetitive rhythm of overhead dryers introduces sculptural forms into the technologically sophisticated color room in the Bumble university.

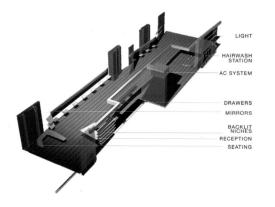

LIGHT

HAIRWASH
STATION

AC SYSTEM

DRAWERS

MIRRORS

BACKLIT
NICHES

RECEPTION

SEATING

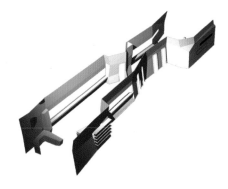

Exploded axonometric concept
drawing

ARCHI-TECTONICS

AIDA'S HOUSE OF BEAUTY
NEW YORK

Amidst the requisite buttoned-down brown-stones on a side street in Manhattan's conservative Upper East Side, Aida's House of Beauty looks as if it might have touched down from another planet. For all its modern drama at first glance, however, the tightly conceived space is truly a study in subtlety. By virtue of maintaining the scale of its neighbors, the new bluestone façade for the deep and narrow space doesn't actually disturb its proper surroundings, just provoke them—the architectural equivalent there of, say, wearing white after Labor Day.

Architect Winka Dubbeldam, of Archi-Tectonics, has been raising academic eyebrows for a decade with her inventive theories. Seeing some of them realized in a succinct, 2,000-square-foot (186-square-meter) endeavor like Aida is cause for celebration. A small scissors-and-comb motif on the salon's exterior recalls shop signs from centuries past. Here, it also foreshadows an interest in the deformation of the volume inside, which appears cut and folded, like a sophisticated origami vertebrate. In creating the carefully sculpted void, a series of wrapping and folding operations have rendered the salon's interior flanking walls "smart;" that is, they embody a system that integrates innovative lighting, heating and cooling equipment, plus sound and storage components. The stark white surfaces focus attention on where each of the planes is joined. Their seams, articulated with crisp mitered edges, become almost ornamental in the spare composition.

The dramatic façade acts as a transparent interface with the street outside, drawing people in and making the street life part of the salon. The plan for the space blooms at the entry and rear, clearly revealing its intention that these areas function in a more social capacity; an inviting garden in the back houses clients in the warm months while they wait their turns. Because the savvy design encourages, above all, a smoothly functioning environment, the salon may be enjoyed by those who know nothing about architectural theory. Perhaps it is fitting that the receptionist has no idea who designed the place, or even that this elegant and sophisticated space is remarkable for its thoughtful concept.

A simple gesture speaks volumes, literally, as the heavy bluestone wall of the façade accepts the glass window and door without fanfare, and the whole is visually realized as the sum of its parts.

Opposite: The deformed walls of the wide corridor looking toward the street suggest natural structures such as caverns or underwater reef walls.

Just inside the door, the walls of the anteroom fold to create a waiting alcove for clients.

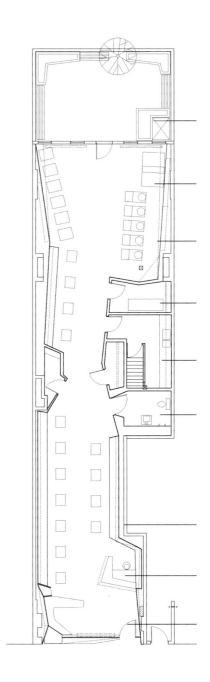

Horizontal mirrored panels over
the symmetric cutting stations
along either wall suggest an infi-
nite number of interactions.

This detail of the sandblasted glass-topped reception desk with empty display shelves behind it aptly demonstrates the joining and deformation operations that characterize the space at large.

THE ARCHITECTURE COMPANY

BABE NAIL & FACE PLACE
DUBLIN

Irish supermodel turned public relations maven Annemarie Gannon was the client for Ireland's first salon dedicated to manicures and pedicures. Babe is located on Drury Street in the prominent urban block that houses the St. George Arcade. This area of Dublin, which formerly catered to the wholesale rag trade, has expanded into the retail market and now also features vegetarian restaurants and tattoo parlors—an ideal spot for the salon's MTV-reared clientele. The small, ornate brick building housing the shop dates from 1890, when it served as a pig abattoir. Offices occupy the top story and a car park the basement, while Babe takes in the ground floor and the level above.

The first move by architects Kealan McCluskey and Georgina Mullen for the 1,060-square-foot (98.5-square-meter) space was to simplify a chopped-up window scheme from the 1970s by substituting a single large storefront window to provide maximum visibility for passersby. Inside, they conceived the design for the salon as a white box that was meant to be playful rather than sterile, or in McCluskey's apt words, "foxy." To this end, the pair created a curved, floor-to-ceiling pink velvet wall element, which occurs on both levels and hides the path of the staircase while neatly organizing the spaces. Walls, ceiling, egg chairs, pendant lamp shades, and linoleum floor remain white to enhance the contrast. The lush texture of the velvet plays off of the smooth leather of the chairs and the shiny chrome throughout, making for an environment that is downright girlie. No doubt, the gay atmosphere created by the vibrant wall has also served as inspiration for the polish on many a Dublin toenail.

Well-lit, custom-designed shelving near the ground-floor reception desk displays products for sale and use in this ultra-mod gathering spot.

Disco balls lend a party air to the pink velvet wall that embraces a pedicure station upstairs.

The funky environment of
Dublin's first manicure salon has
been so successful that it has
spawned others throughout
the capital city.

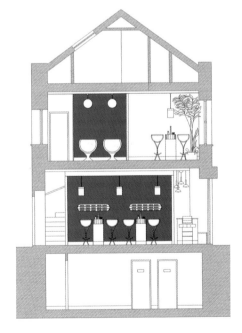

Section showing pink walls on each level

A mirrored wall running along the rear of the relatively tight upstairs space helps to open up the "white box" scheme.

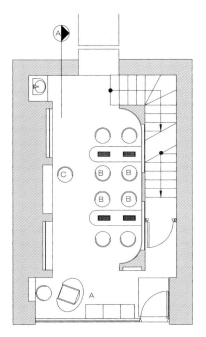

Plan of ground level

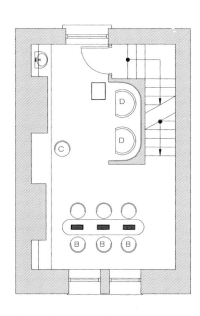

Plan of upper level

turquoise, rose, and violet light leak over the walls of the cubelike spaces and bleed into the reception and waiting areas, bathing these otherwise stark modernist environments in a glow of ethereal tones.

The symmetry of this conceit is fairly breathtaking, reminding us of the very nature of light, which exists without boundaries until contained, when it lends definition to space by carving it out perceptually. The worldwide design community has recognized the peculiar beauty of these spaces: a recent retrospective at the Cooper-Hewitt, National Design Museum compared compared the Electric Sun designers, Frank Escher and Ravi GuneWardena, to none other than Mies van der Rohe for their streamlined offerings.

The design of Electric Sun I was driven in part by the client's wish to monitor the activity of the entire 3,500-square-foot (325-square-meter) salon from the waiting area and by the air handling needs of high-capacity equipment that affected the air conditioning of the overall volume. But the shifting play of light from the tanning booths as the beds turn on or off formed the central definition of space. For Electric Sun II, the next evolution in this series of light studies, the architects introduced transparent materials such as gauzy curtains and acrylic forms. Their third and most oddly elegant salon, Electric Sun III, takes the interchange of light a step further. High-intensity tanning beds cast a deep blue glaze over the solid walls at the rear. For its street front, the architects wanted to create a graphic response to the billboards that abound at the salon's location in a mini-mall across from the famed Beverly Center. They collaborated with the artist Jonathan Williams on a series of translucent acrylic tanning booths adorned in large-scale graphics depicting organic plant material. Set before the windows that wrap around the second-story space, they function as colorful lanterns when in use, beckoning to the street life below.

The graffiti-clad Electric Sun III contributes its own graphic message to the streetscape, echoing the billboards at the intersection of La Cienega and Beverly Boulevards.

ESCHER GUNEWARDENA ARCHITECTURE

ELECTRIC SUN I, II, III
LOS ANGELES

In the case of the designs for three Electric Sun tanning salons in Los Angeles, form follows function so purely it's actually a bit eerie, as well as staggeringly beautiful. When patrons use the tanning beds, washes of

Richly chromatic, hyperreal flowers and vines adorn the outsides of acrylic tanning booths in Electric Sun III.

The reception area of Electric Sun I, a salon with eighteen tanning booths, features furniture designed as sculptural objects floating within the tranquil environment. The strict composition is like an abstract color-field painting made three-dimensional.

Rose-colored light emanating from a tanning cubicle in Electric Sun I spreads up the walls and onto the crisp white ceiling in the hallway, creating a kind of second sun.

Opposite: Light and shadow play across the walls and cubelike volumes of Electric Sun I.

The regularity of the white cubistic volumes in the public areas at Electric Sun III is both highlighted and softened by light seeping in from the private zones.

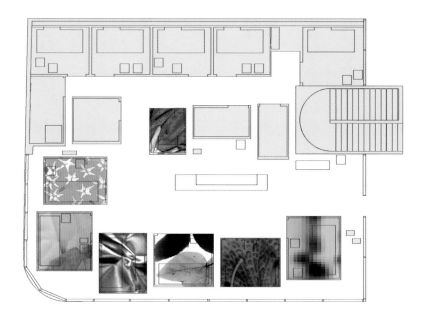

Floor plan of Electric Sun III

This hypnotic blue hallway in Electric Sun III, bathed in light from an unknown source, suggests a scene from a science fiction movie.

FUMITA DESIGN OFFICE

STAR GARDEN BEAUTY SALON & HEALTH SPA TOKYO

Opposite: A series of grids of widely varying scales and in contrasting materials creates a dynamic composition in the first-floor area that houses the shampoo bar and cashier.

The custom-designed shampoo dispensers feature stainless metal tubes indicating where to position containers and also catch occasional spills.

With such diverse offerings as a shampoo bar, teeth whitening facilities, chairs for head and foot massages, and mobile hair styling stations dispersed across three floors, this 11,560 square-foot (1,074-square-meter) project could easily have suffered from design schizophrenia or overkill. On the contrary: Akihito Fumita's Tokyo design for Natural Body, a Japanese chain of beauty and health complexes, displays a felicitous marriage of pageantry and supremely inventive technology. It's clean without being clinical, and sophisticated but far from stuffy. The name Star Garden refers to the salon's luminous results. The exclusively female clientele are made to feel like celebrities after their various treatments, and to this end a ceremonial circular stair links the three levels; the final stop for each guest is a turn down the lower staircase, where a camera from the on-site digital photo studio documents her transformation.

Designed as a collection of boutiques such as one might encounter in a high-end department store, the spaces dedicated to separate beauty functions are nonetheless visually connected throughout the three open plans. A spare material palette helps achieve this continuity. Glass features most prominently: Its applications include the blue-tinted freestanding shelving lined with varieties of mineral water that surrounds the first-floor shampoo bar (the joints are secured by adhesive) and the floor-to-ceiling walls that divide areas for VIP clients—on the second floor for massages and on the third for hair styling sessions. Stainless steel is also used to convey a hyper-modern—in the sense of extremely functional—sensibility. It characterizes the shampoo bar, where clients may select from twenty formulas and bring their own bottles for refills, as well as the stands for the mobile mirrors on both the first and third floors. A white tile floor anchors the first level, and pale carpet the second, whereas the upper level signals a significant aesthetic departure by virtue of its dark hardwood. One welcome measure of whimsy in the clean spaces is the suggestive silhouettes of the massage chairs, some of which are shaped like rabbits' ears. It is in the hair salon, however, that Fumita's most entertaining gesture awaits: eighteenth-century European drawing room chairs upholstered in colorful graphic fabrics with philosophical messages in French are convened like old friends. Alongside, the straight bones of the rolling mirrors perfectly complement their companions' lush curves.

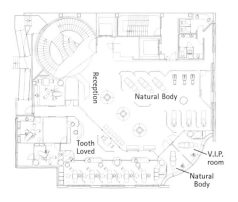

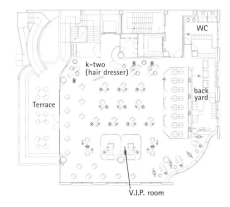

Plans of first, second, and third floors

In one example of the salon's innovative lighting, flexible tubing houses curved fluorescent lamps imbedded in mobile makeup mirrors.

Saucerlike discs hovering from the second-floor ceiling provide ambient light for the relaxed massage patrons; they also house (and hide) the room's ventilation system.

Beyond the glass-partitioned public zone, ceiling cutouts accommodate a serpentine wall behind which guests to Toothed Love dental clinic receive orthodontic and cosmetic treatments.

A sensational balance of formality and whimsy, functionality and comfort is expressed in the fluid furniture plan of K-Two, the hair styling boutique.

Translucent curved glass walls, which give back reflected light, delineate private styling cabins on the third floor.

Even with the drying bonnet, this sleek, industrial scene is a world apart from the traditional beauty parlor décor of decades past.

JPDA AND MESH ARCHITECTURES

OSCAR BOND SALON NEW YORK

"The Jetsons meets Barbarella" was the briefest of design proposals that sold the salon client on this collaboration by Eric Liftin of MESH Architectures and Jordan Parnass of JPDA (Jordan Parnass Digital Architecture), two Columbia architecture school friends. True to their vision, the 3,500-square-foot (325-square-meter) space in a Soho basement is both dramatic and streamlined, with suspended iMacs setting the (orange vinyl-upholstered) stage in the waiting area. But this tells only half the story. The Oscar Bond Salon is also an oddly elegant space, owing, ironically, to its limited design budget: a mere $200,000 (£107,039).

Exposed I-beams, ductwork, and plumbing apparatuses on the ceiling, as well as a central row of six untreated cast-iron columns that runs the length of the rectangular space lend a welcome sense of utility and grace to the salon's otherwise retro-futuristic atmosphere. Backlit orange-and-white nylon parachute fabric covers the walls to economize over drywall and soften what could have amounted to subterranean gloom. This solution also offers hidden storage space.

The broader concept of a salon as a place for social gathering and exchange served as the central source of inspiration for Oscar Bond's young designers. These connections occur both actually and virtually. Clients enter the space on a "runway" staircase from which they survey the scene while being seen. At the reception desk, a webcam records each patron's image and sends it out over the Internet, linking the salon's virtual and physical sites. Video monitors relay recorded and live images above the reception area and the waiting platform in the middle of the space. Two net-connected computers suspended over this elevated stage make it not only a place to engage with others sitting there, but an ideal environment to check email and participate in a wider source of culture outside the walls of the salon.

A defining element of the space is a long shallow staircase that prolongs the event of entry, depositing incoming guests past the retail product display and well into the space.

The aesthetic of the relaxed yet composed reception area announces the material mixture of heavy and buoyant, raw and refined that is continued throughout.

Opposite: Diffused fluorescent light seeps from overhead panels and from beneath the raised floor in the elevated waiting area that functions as the salon's nexus.

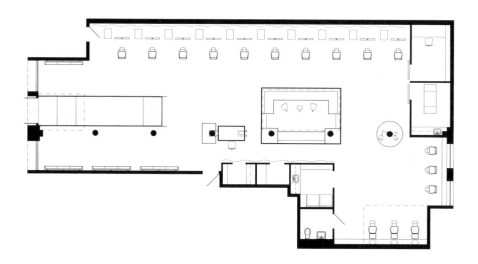

An ingenious overhead light fixture made from plumbing pipes is repeated to great effect along the bank of cutting stations that runs the length of the wall.

Opposite: A pebbled glass sliding door at the rear of the space separates the single treatment room, adorned in uncharacteristically cool colors, from the remainder of the salon.

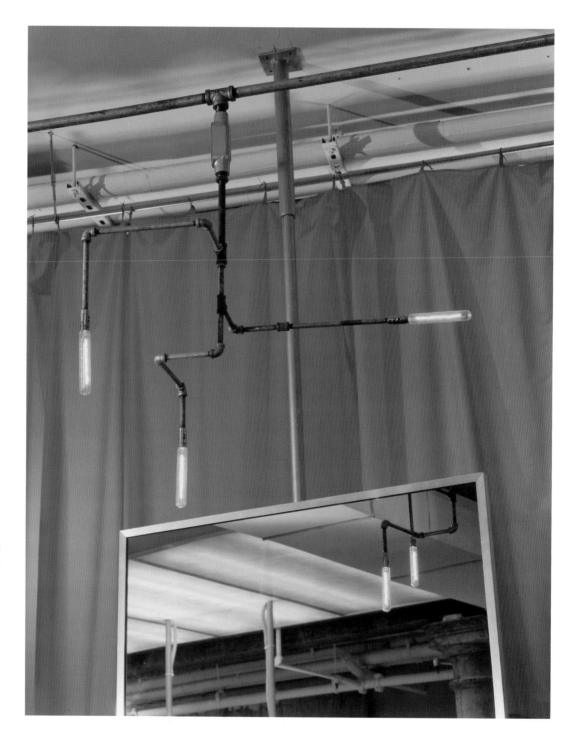

JUMP STUDIOS

LYNX BARBERSHOP LONDON

That the design for London's Lynx Barbershop has been compared with Stanley Kubrick's interior sets for *A Clockwork Orange*, the cinematic watershed event from the early 1970s, makes perfect sense. The environments share technological savvy, a love for soft-edged, predominantly rounded forms and reflective, man-made materials, and were created as spaces to indulge men, pure and simple. That the world of cinema is literally incorporated into the haircutting experience here makes the analogy even more.

Jump Studios architects Shaun Fernandes and Simon Jordan turned the concept of the traditional salon on its head by taking their design cues for this 1,000-square-foot (93-square-meter) space from bars and clubs—the very places that the young men who make up the barbershop's clientele would elect to be. There's no embarrassing parade in a goofy plastic cape around this long space: All salon functions are accommodated at eight semiprivate individual stations serviced by fiberglass pods that house a swing-out sink, mirror, product display space, and even plasma screens for viewing a favorite movie or music video. Rubber-tile floors provide a comfortable surface for the stylists in addition to deadening sounds that might violate a proper viewing experience.

Near the entrance, patrons wait their turn in a "break-out" zone that offers the latest in Playstation and GameBoy technology, plus underground magazines from around the world. This is not anyone's father's barbershop, but lest these young gentlemen forget where they are, two vibrantly painted red and white striped floor-to-ceiling "barber poles" in the reception area serve to remind them.

The masculine palette of black, white, and gray conjures an appropriate attitude of bespoke pinstripes, with an ersatz barber's pole lending a proper red accent.

Opposite: This tightly controlled design depends on details such as the repetitive circular motifs of the ceiling and floor lights.

Young male patrons are encouraged to feel at home in the waiting area with a wealth of interactive games at their disposal.

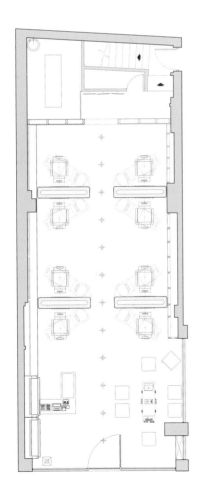

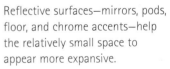

Reflective surfaces—mirrors, pods, floor, and chrome accents—help the relatively small space to appear more expansive.

The clean composition of 6 Salon's exterior features a frosted glass clerestory obscuring a dropped ceiling, above which is housed a robust mechanical system. Apartments on the building's upper floors prevented roof access.

M1/DTW

6 SALON ROYAL OAK

The clients for 6 Salon insisted that good light be the design priority for their new space in a small, culturally rich community north of Detroit. (In their former location they had escorted patrons out to the sidewalk to check on the progress of coloring applications.) So light they got, in the form of over two hundred artificial lamps and an

entirely open glazed, east-facing façade that wraps around the corner to form an entry and garner some southern exposure as well. The creative process is still a public event, this time in the form of live video images of salon activities broadcast to passersby on a band of LED monitors placed street side.

The project's young designers, Christian Unverzagt and Chris Benfield of M1/DTW, describe themselves as interested in the intersection of design, digital technology, and small-scale manufacturing. Embarking on the project for 6 Salon, they were "looking to transgress the disciplinary boundaries of their skills, interests, and abilities." Their work encompasses the salon's graphics and website as well as its three-dimensional expression. The team harbored no preconceptions about what was possible—producing an interior that is both vital and serene, with a sophisticated palette of materials and metaphors.

A mandate for light meant that the two existing columns in the 2,800-square-foot (260-square-meter) former record store would provide the essential interior structure and allow for a space unobstructed by weight-bearing partitions. Beginning with the eastern façade, a layering of parallel walls organizes and divides the open expanse. This translucent, vertical exterior plane is visually echoed halfway into the space by two softly diffuse chain mail mesh curtains (which, incidentally, contain and serve almost to dissolve the columns). Another 34-foot (10.5-meter)-long wall of eleven glass panels rises from dropped floor to dropped ceiling. Just 18 inches (46 centimeters) from the room's boundary and only $^3/_4$ inch (2 centimeters) thick, its backlit, sandblasted finish lends it an ethereal presence and suggests the promise of something beyond. Rather than the plethora of salons and wig shops that line the avenues of the nearby inner city, these clean, linear elements recall the vocabularies of gallery spaces. Here, however, it is the techniques of the stylists and the participation of the clients in the act of image making that are on view.

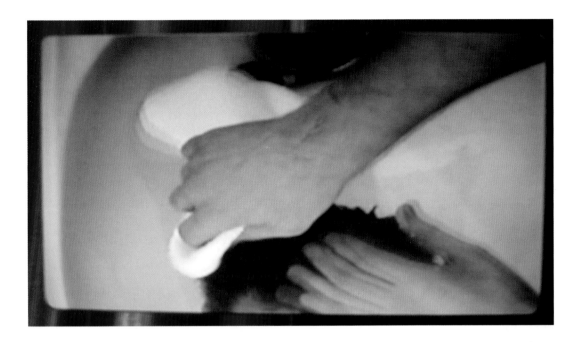

The live video feed of salon activities is tightly cropped to convey precise moments of contact between the stylist and client.

Below: Self-supporting, backlit, sandblasted glass panels were inserted into a 1-$\frac{1}{2}$-inch (3.4-centimeter) U-shaped channel in the dropped floor. A parade of suspended stainless steel stations, containing mirrors and built-in supply drawers, were custom designed to further free the ground plane.

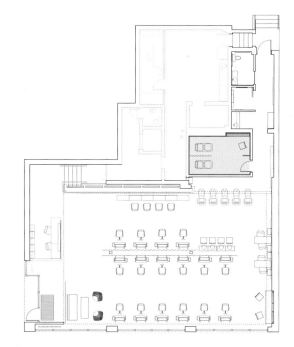

"In coming here, you agree to participate," explains designer Christian Unverzagt, pointing to styling chairs lined up in front of the windows, where they serve as advertising. A further bounty of this arrangement is the soft rhythm of ever-changing shadows across the floor.

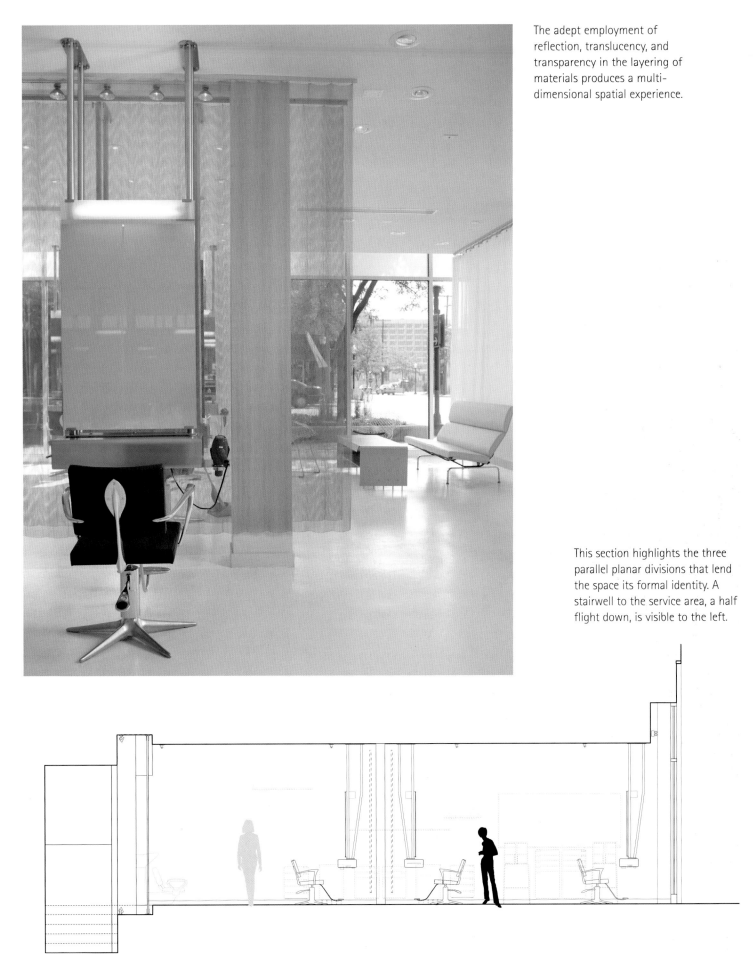

The adept employment of reflection, translucency, and transparency in the layering of materials produces a multi-dimensional spatial experience.

This section highlights the three parallel planar divisions that lend the space its formal identity. A stairwell to the service area, a half flight down, is visible to the left.

PETERSEN + VERWERS ARCHITECTURE

ELEVATION SALON + CAFÉ
SAN FRANCISCO

Opposite: The capsule-shaped reception desk in the long narrow entry contains the requisite product display. This space introduces the spare palette—white, dove grey, and dusty blue—employed throughout the salon.

The cylinder that houses the café wraps around to provide a semi-private consultation area.

The "kitchen" is the old term for the place within a beauty parlor where the color is mixed. Fortunately for its guests, this reductive design for a San Francisco hair salon and café separates the two activities. Located in the Financial District, Elevation is the city's largest street-level salon, with twenty-eight stations in an expansive 3,365-square-foot (312.5-square-meter) space. As the name suggests, the beauty experience here is meant to be uplifting. And it is, by all accounts from those who've stopped in to drink a soy cappuccino or view a Dolce & Gabbana runway collection before or after a first-rate primping appointment.

Essentially one large rectilinear room, with service areas arranged behind partitions along a back wall, openness and visibility characterize the minimally elegant space. Well-considered lighting helps to achieve this ideal. The back wall, which faces an alley, is lined with translucent glass windows that admit plenty of daylight while hiding an unappealing view. California's Title 24 Energy Code requires that a salon's primary lights be fluorescent; to accommodate his desire that the 14-foot (4-meter) ceiling seem even higher, architect Todd Verwers cleverly concealed a series of up-lighting tubes in stainless steel fixtures mounted along perimeter walls and above the café area. Wide mirrors along the side walls provide more visibility.

While maintaining a clean, crisp atmosphere meant relegating most hairstyling implements to custom-designed drawers at each station, considerations for comfort and ease of function were paramount. In the washing area, for instance, freestanding sinks allow workers to massage and shampoo their client's scalps without contorting their own bodies. Rubber mats are sunk down into a concrete floor scored with grooves, so that stylists' feet and legs don't take the brunt of their long day's efforts.

The focal point of the salon is the cylindrical café measuring 15 feet (4.5 meters) in diameter. Here stylists, clients, and even waiting friends of clients meet over lattes. The round form generates easy communication by providing a more encompassing view of the active proceedings to either side. Indeed, Verwers sees his design's most spectacular feature as a "theatrical venue for salon life."

The centrally located café serves as a meeting place for stylists and clients to discuss their creations; its round form heightens our awareness of the otherwise rectilinear plan.

A make-up station near the reception desk features falls made of genuine hair.

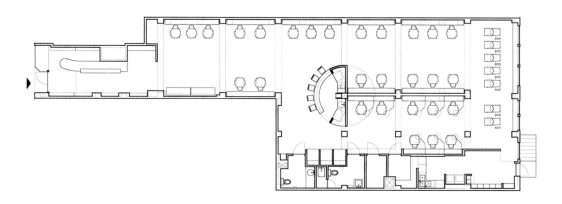

Left: Diffused light floods into the washing area through windows facing a back alley.

The salon's spatial arrangement derives from the rhythm of existing columns augmented by rectilinear inserts relieved by the rounded café form.

Long, horizontal mirrors above the coloring stations help to direct the gaze of passersby and entering patrons toward the rear of the space.

Opposite: Fluorescent ceiling tubes continue the linear gesture of the mirrors on a different plane.

SAUCIER + PERROTTE ARCHITECTES

ORBITE HAIR SALON
MONTRÉAL

For a decade now, Orbite's dramatic hair designs have been ahead of the pack in relation to its Canadian competitors. The revamping of the salon, then, somehow needed to reinforce this image. But fashion and architecture have very different production schedules—and shelf lives. Rather than provide a design that would be deemed *outré* the next season, Montréal architects Gilles Saucier and André Perrotte came up with a

cerebral solution of classic modernism as the perfect backdrop for artful experimentation.

An inherited U-shaped plan is configured around a sizable condominium entrance that divides two large street-front windows. The duo was faced with creating a sense of continuity between the façades (and exploiting the opportunity for theatricality) while affording some privacy for clients inside. In this case, the final design of the space displays a clear evolution from the original conceptual sketches.

The 2,150-square-foot (200-square-meter) space telescopes, meaning the sidewalls project into the room increasingly as the space recedes toward the back. At each point where the winnowing occurs, there's a visible cut in the walls from which emanates a strip of vivid colored light. The salon's austere white, black, and gray palette is augmented in this way by bands of taxicab yellow; large glass screens in vivid crimson demarcate private zones within the open space. Long slender mirrors are oriented horizontally along tables in the coloring area and are suspended vertically in the cutting and styling zones. The mirrors, like other lean elements such as the dark incisions in the floor, underscore the strong sense of linearity that characterizes the pristine interior. The impressive spatial effect of these reflective slices, however, is to suggest a parallel but altogether different sense of depth, confounding us about interior/exterior divisions by bringing the outdoors directly into the space; in this way, the mirrors may be understood to be producing their own telescoping exercise. What results is a fragmented reality not unlike that of an experimental stage set, which is a most fitting analogy for this site of ultimate drama.

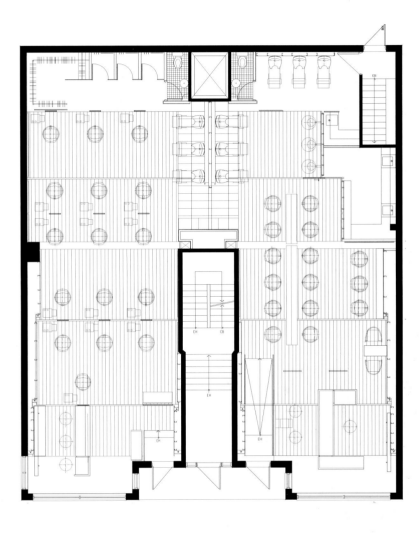

The symmetry of the plan is reinforced by the placement of elements such as these vertically oriented mirrors.

In the reception area, stainless steel fixtures and precise planes of red shelving aid in the salon's overall sense of clinical precision.

Diagrammatic conceptual sketch of light and space

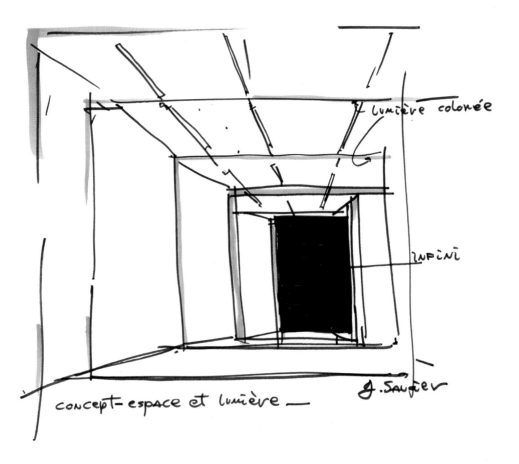

lumière colorée

INFINI

concept–espace et lumière —

J. Sautier

A ruby-colored glass screen offers privacy for those who might feel vulnerable when undergoing treatments.

Vertical strip mirrors hanging
against a mirror wall dissolve
space and contribute to a feeling
of uncanniness.

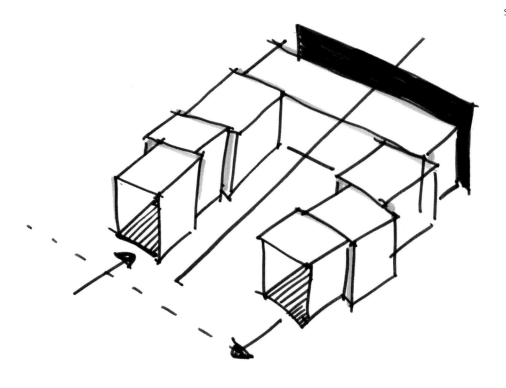

Diagrammatic conceptual sketch of the salon's telescoping geometry

The intersecting lines of the handrail and colorful wall joint against a clean white background bring to mind the spatial paintings of Piet Mondrian.

DIRECTORY OF ARCHITECTS AND DESIGNERS

3SIX0
112 Union St., Suite 303
Providence, RI 02903
United States
401.421.4360
www.3six0.com

Abramson Teiger Architects
8924 Lindblade St.
Culver City, CA 90232
United States
310.838.8998
www.abramsonteiger.com

anderson architects
555 West 25th St.
New York, NY 10001
United States
212.630.0996
www.andersonarch.com

Archi-Tectonics
200 Varick St., Suite 507b
New York, NY 10014
United States
212.206.0920
www.archi-tectonics.com

The Architecture Company
42 Upper Dominick St.
Dublin 7
Ireland
1.860.3150

ARO (Architecture Research Office)
180 Varick St., 10th floor
New York, NY 10014
United States
212.675.1870
www.aro.net

Jacqueline and Henri Boiffils
44 rue d'Assas
75006 Paris
France
1.4284.2000
www.boiffils.com

burdifilek
183 Bathurst St., Suite 300
Toronto, Ontario
M5T 2R7
Canada
416.703.4334

Clodagh Design
670 Broadway, 4th floor
New York, NY 10012
United States
212.780.5300
www.clodagh.com

Desai/Chia Studio
54 West 21st St., 7th floor
New York, NY 10010
United States
212.366.9630
www.desaichia.com

DMAC Architecture
800 West Evergreen Ave.
Chicago, IL 60622
United States
312.573.1237

Emmanuelle Duplay
174 Quai de Jemmapes
75010 Paris
France
1.4018.5950

Escher GuneWardena Architects
815 Silver Lake Blvd.
Los Angeles, CA 90026
United States
323.665.9100
www.eschergunewardena.com

Fumita Design Office
2-18-2 Minami Aoyama
Minato ku, Tokyo 107-0062
Japan
81.3.5414.2880
www.fumitadesign.com

Grimshaw
1 Conway St.
Fitzroy Square
London W1T 6LR
United Kingdom
20.7291.4141
www.grimshaw-architects.com

Groves Natcheva Architects
38 Gloucester Rd.
London SW7 4QT
United Kingdom
20.7823.8804
www.grovesnatcheva.com

JPDA (Jordan Parnass Digital Architecture)
68 Jay St., no. 301A
Brooklyn, NY 11201
United States
718.852.2650
www.jpda.net

Jump Studios
35 Britannia Row
London N1 8QH
United Kingdom
20.7688.0080
www.jump-studios.com

M1/DTW
1604 Clay Ave., 3rd floor
Detroit, MI 48211
United States
313.874.5936
www.m1dtw.com

MSH Design
23815 Northwoods View Rd.
West Hills, CA 93107
United States
310.251.9935
www.mshdesign.com

MESH Architectures
180 Varick St., 11th floor
New York, NY 10014
United States
212.989.3884
www.mesh-arc.com

Molnar Freeman Architects
14 Moncur St.
Woollahra NSW 2025
Australia
2.9327.1926
www.molnarfreeman.com

Office dA
57 East Concord St., no. 6
Boston, MA 02118
United States
617.267.7369
www.officeda.com

Petersen + Verwers Architecture
2325 Third St., Suite 204
San Francisco, CA 94107
United States
415.734.9669
www.petersenverwers.com

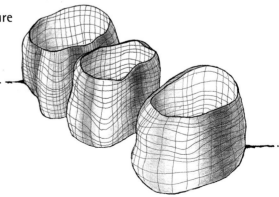

DIRECTORY OF SALONS AND SPAS

6 Salon
306 West Sixth St.
Royal Oak, MI 48067
United States
248.398.1586

Aida's House of Beauty
209 East 76th St.
New York, NY 10021
United States
212.228.1020

Babe Nail & Face Place
Dublin
Ireland

Bumble and bumble.Salon
415 West 13th St.
New York, NY 10014
United States
212.521.6500
www.bumbleandbumble.com

Calmia Day Spa
52–54 Marylebone High St.
London W1U 5HR
United Kingdom
20.7224.3585
www.calmia.com

Calmia at Selfridges
400 Duke St.
London W1 1AB
United Kingdom
84.5009.2450
www.calmia.com

Clear Spa and Salon
300 York Mills Rd.
Toronto, Ontario
M2L 2Y5
Canada
416.386.0350

Dermalogica on Montana
1022 Montana Ave.
Santa Monica, CA 90404
United States
310.260.8682

Electric Sun III
8471 Beverly Blvd.
Los Angeles, CA 90048
United States
310.966.3100

Elevation Salon + Café
451 Bush St.
San Francisco, CA 94108
United States
415.392.2969
www.elevationsalon.com

Iunx Parfumerie
48-50 rue de l'Université
75007 Paris
France
1.4544.5014

James Joseph Salon
30 Newbury St.
Boston, MA 02116
United States
617.266.7222
www.jamesjosephsalon.com

Joli Hair Design
185 Grove St.
Chestnut Hill, MA 02467
United States
617.327.0900

LabulleKenzo
1 rue du Pont Neuf
75001 Paris
France
1.7304.2004

Lumière Salon
57 Eddy St.
Providence, RI 02903
United States
401.521.2777
www.lumieresalon.com

Lynx Barbershop
19 Market Place
Kingston-upon-Thames
London KT1 1EU
United Kingdom
20.8541.8375

Mario Tricoci Salon & Day Spa
900 North Michigan Ave.
Chicago, IL 60611
United States
312.915.0960
www.tricoci.com

Orbite Salon
215 Laurier Ave. West
Montréal, Québec
H2T 2N9
Canada
514.271.6333

Oscar Bond Salon
42 Wooster St.
New York, NY 10013
United States
212.334.3777
www.oscarbondsalon.com

Prema Nolita Day Spa
New York
United States

Qiora Store and Spa
New York
United States

Ryuko Hasshin Hair Salon
2-3-4 Toride
Toride-shi, Ibaraki Prefecture 302-0004
Japan
81.0297.71.3938

Sally Hershberger at John Freida
8440 Melrose Place
Los Angeles, CA 90069
United States
323.653.4040

Sasanqua Day Spa
Kiawah Island Club
10 River Course Lane
Kiawah Island, SC 29455
United States
843.768.2582

Star Garden Beauty Salon & Health Spa
1-5-4 Shoto
Shibuya-ku, Tokyo 150-0000
Japan
81.3.3496.8739

Thermae Bath Spa
Hot Bath St.
Bath BA1 1SJ
United Kingdom
1225.33.5678

Wink! Hair Salon
50-58 Hunter St.
Sydney NSW 2000
Australia
2.9222.2899

PHOTOGRAPHER CREDITS

Marc Abel
Pages 8 (bottom), 38–45

anderson architects
Pages 88, 104

Daniel Aubry
Page 86

Dan Bibb
Pages 82–85

Michael Boone
Pages 13 (bottom), 37

Calmia Ltd.
Page 60

Marc Cramer
Pages 154–161

John Ellis
Pages 11 (bottom), 120, 121, 126, 127, 167

Lars Frazer
Pages 98, 100–103

Francis Giacobetti
Pages 12, 20–23

Groves Natcheva Architects
Pages 6, 7, 58, 59, 61–63

GTODD Photography
Pages 144–147

Patrick Bingham Hall
Pages 64–67

John Horner
Pages 5, 76–81, 87, 91–97

David Joseph
Pages 15–19

John Edward Linden
Page 99

Michael Lisnet
Pages 105–109

Joshua McHugh
Pages 30–33

Michael Moran / www.moranstudio.com
Pages 9, 89, 134–139

Nacása & Partners Inc.
Pages 46–49, 128–133

Con O'Donoghue
Pages 116–119

Greg Ogami
Pages 122–124, 125 (top)

Petersen + Verwers Architecture
Pages 88, 148–153

Ben Rahn
Pages 11 (top), 24–29

Doug Snower
Pages 34–36

Tim Street-Porter
Pages 13 (top), 68–75

Studio Lipnitski/Courtesy of Helena
Rubinstein Foundation, 8 (top)

Edmund Sumner
Pages 10, 51–54, 56, 57

Paul Warchol
Pages 111–115

Mark York
Pages 140–143

ACKNOWLEDGMENTS

My thanks to each of the architects, designers, and photographers featured in the book. Your work was inspiring and your assistance in representing it invaluable. I am equally indebted to your office colleagues who were unflagging in their enthusiastic aid. To my friends who are tireless in their willingness to share ideas, I am always profoundly thankful. Betsy Gammons deserves special praise for her continual guidance and assurance. I owe the concept for the book to Alicia Kennedy, my editor, and remain ever grateful for your insightful critiques and exacting art direction. And finally, to those who have encouraged me to search for beauty in less obvious places, there will be other books.

ABOUT THE AUTHOR

Photo: Olive Beasley

Julie Sinclair Eakin writes about design. She has advanced degrees in architecture from SCI-Arc and the University of California at Berkeley. Her writing has appeared in the *New York Times* and the *Los Angeles Times.* She lives in New York City. This is her first book.